W9-AAH-386

Microsoft®
Exchange Server Resource Guide, Supplement

Microsoft Press

PUBLISHED BY
Microsoft Press
A Division of Microsoft Corporation
One Microsoft Way
Redmond, Washington 98052-6399

Copyright © 1997 by Microsoft Corporation

Library of Congress Cataloging-in-Publication Data
Microsoft BackOffice Resource Kit, Part Two / Microsoft Corporation.
     p.   cm.
   Includes index.
   ISBN 1-57231-534-2
   1. Microsoft BackOffice.   2. Client/server computing.
  I. Microsoft Corporation.
  QA76.9.C55M52   1997
  005.7'1376--dc21   97-831
                                                  CIP

Printed and bound in the United States of America.

1 2 3 4 5 6 7 8 9 WCWC 2 1 0 9 8 7

Distributed to the book trade in Canada by Macmillan of Canada, a division of Canada Publishing Corporation.

A CIP catalogue record for this book is available from the British Library.

Microsoft Press books are available through booksellers and distributors worldwide. For further information about international editions, contact your local Microsoft Corporation office. Or contact Microsoft Press International directly at fax (206) 936-7329.

Acquisitions Editor: Casey D. Doyle
Project Editor: Stuart J. Stuple

Part No. 097-0001789 (Microsoft Exchange Server Resource Guide, Supplement)

This book is dedicated to all the hard working writers, editors, reviewers, and numerous production staff people at Microsoft who make books like this possible. Thank you!

Contributors to this book include the following:

Contributing Writers

Scott Briggs, Kali Buhariwalla, Jim Chismar, Sukvinder Singh Gill, Brian Mahoney, Joseph Pagano, Joseph Roberts, Rob Sanfilippo, Eric Savoldi, Dean Simpson, Len Wyatt

Technical Consultants

Susan Nellis, Steven Bailey, John Baker, Michael Bird, Adam Blum, Scott Briggs, Kali Buhariwalla, John Coleman, Rick Cook, KC Cross, Andrei Davydov, Tom DeFeo, Jaime Emmanuelli, Alan Erickson, Ken Ewert, Ian Farrell, Deb Ferrell, Bob Gering, Rob P. Gilmore, David Goodhand, Robert Hughes, Phillip Hupf, Brent Jensen, Martin Kohlleppel, John Kozell, Elizabeth Kutler, Johnny Lee, Stephen Leverett, Eric Lockard, Ann McCurdy, Thomas McInerney, Tony Meleg, Paul Moore, Patti Moree, Brian Murphy, Mahesh Nasta, Noel O'Flarity, Joe Orzech, Scott Paulson, Vanitha Prabhakaran, Mark Pustilnik, Jim Reitz, Tom Rizzo, Joseph Roberts, Angela Schmeil, Joel Soderberg, Andrzej Turski, Jithendra Veeramachaneni, Edmond VonAllmen, Dick Vorhees, Daniel Weisman, Cathy Westman

Technical Writer
Candy Paape

Technical Editors
Connie La Chasse, Sharon Farrar

Contents

Introduction

Welcome to the *Microsoft Exchange Server Resource Guide, Supplement One*. This guide is designed for people who are, or who want to become, expert users of Microsoft® Exchange Server and Microsoft Exchange Client.

The *Microsoft Exchange Server Resource Guide, Supplement One* is a technical supplement to the documentation included as part of the Microsoft Exchange Server product and does not replace that information as the source for learning how to use Microsoft Exchange Server.

About the Resource Guide

This guide includes the following chapters:

Chapter 1, "Planning and Setup," explains how to plan for efficiently adding users to Microsoft Exchange Server. It also describes the factors affecting performance and how to automate the installation process.

Chapter 2, "Working with Microsoft Exchange Server," describes how to maintain Microsoft Exchange Server and Microsoft Exchange Client. It includes information about using Russian, Eastern European, Greek and Turkish language character sets, Message Transfer Agent (MTA) routing, and procedures for moving Microsoft Exchange Server to another computer.

Chapter 3, "Optimizing Performance," discusses how to optimize the performance of Microsoft Exchange Server by balancing server and hardware resources, and by adjusting software settings.

Chapter 4, "Microsoft Exchange Server Disaster Recovery," describes data recovery techniques that can be applied to Microsoft Exchange Server for the quickest possible data recovery in the event of a system crash or another disaster.

Chapter 5, "Application Development," provides examples of custom solutions that can be developed for Microsoft Exchange Server. Development of custom solutions can range from modifying existing sample applications to using high-end development tools to create more complex groupware applications.

Chapter 6, "Microsoft Exchange Server Registry Reference," identifies registry values that can be used to configure Microsoft Exchange Server.

Chapter 7, "Troubleshooting Microsoft Exchange Server," provides information about troubleshooting problems with Microsoft Exchange Server and Microsoft Exchange Client.

Additional Information

Many resources are available that provide additional information about Microsoft Exchange Server.

Microsoft BackOffice Resource Kit, Part Two Compact Disc

The Microsoft BackOffice™ Resource Kit, Part Two compact disc contains Microsoft Exchange Server tools and related online documentation.

Web Sites

Visit the following sites on the World Wide Web for up-to-date information about Microsoft Exchange Server:

http://www.microsoft.com/exchange   The Microsoft Exchange Server Web site contains up-to-date information about Microsoft Exchange Server and links to other Microsoft BackOffice products.

http://www.microsoft.com/syspro/technet/boes/bo/mailexch/exch/tools/appfarm/appfarm1.htm
The Microsoft Exchange Server Application Farm Web site includes sample applications and other development tools that enable you to develop your own applications for Microsoft Exchange Server.

http://www.microsoft.com/support/products/backoffice/msmail.htm
The Microsoft Exchange Server Technical Support Web site gives you access to the Microsoft Exchange Server Knowledge Base, support information, and frequently-asked questions.

http://www.microsoft.com/technet   The Microsoft TechNet Web site contains information about subscribing to Microsoft TechNet, which provides in-depth technical information about Microsoft business products, including Microsoft Exchange Server and other Microsoft BackOffice products.

http://www.microsoft.com/train_cert   The Microsoft Training and Certification Web site provides information about training options and the Microsoft Certified Professional Program.

Conventions in This Manual

The following table summarizes the typographic conventions used in the *Microsoft Exchange Server Resource Guide, Supplement One*.

Convention	Description
bold	Menus and menu commands, command buttons, property page and dialog box titles and options, command-line commands, options, and portions of syntax that must be typed exactly as shown.
Initial Capitals	Names of applications, programs, and named windows.
italic	Information you provide, terms that are being introduced, and book titles.
KEY+KEY	Key combinations in which you press and hold down one key and then press another.
`monospace`	Examples, sample command lines, program code, and program output.
SMALL CAPITALS	Names of keys on the keyboard.

C H A P T E R   1

Planning and Setup

This chapter describes methods to consider when planning your rollout and setting up Microsoft Exchange Server. It also explains how to configure Microsoft Exchange Server to run at optimum performance and how to automate the installation process.

Adding Users to Microsoft Exchange Server

There are a number of performance-related issues involved in adding users to a Microsoft Exchange Server organization.

Users vary widely in their messaging, scheduling, and workgroup usage levels. Individual usage patterns, schedules, and activity levels depend upon the degree to which e-mail, group, and personal scheduling and public folder applications are used for business and personal activities within the organization.

Number of Users Per Server

The main factor in determining the number of users a Microsoft Exchange Server computer can support is the load each user places on the server. This dependency generally falls into two distinct categories: user-initiated actions and background actions.

Some users interact with the server for 12 hours at a time, while others connect to the server only once a week for a few minutes. Some users read hundreds of messages in dozens of public folders every day, while others read none at all. In a given user community, a small percentage of users can generate a disproportionate percentage of the total load on a server because they are the heavier, more aggressive users.

User-Initiated Actions

When a user interacts with the server directly, the actions performed place an immediate incremental load on the server for a duration of time. *User-initiated actions* are operations that the server performs as a direct result of a user's action, and are synchronous from the user's point of view. For example, opening an unread message in a private folder in the server information store entails processing time on the server to receive and interpret the open request. The server must evaluate access restrictions, retrieve the message from the database, mark the message as unread, update the unread count for the folder, return the requested message properties to the client, and generate a folder notification to the client. All of this happens in the time it takes for the remote procedure call (RPC) issued by the Microsoft Exchange Client to return control to the client. The actual time that the user perceives the operation takes is this time, plus the additional processing time needed by the client to draw the window, display the message properties, and so on.

User-initiated actions are the single most important factor in sizing a Microsoft Exchange Server computer. The performance of any given server is directly proportional to the number of users actively interacting with the server per unit time and the actions performed.

Background Actions

In addition to user-initiated actions, Microsoft Exchange Server performs asynchronous or background actions on behalf of users. Accepting, transferring and delivering messages, making routing decisions, expanding distribution lists, replicating changes to public folders and directory service information, executing rules, monitoring storage quotas, and performing background maintenance such as deleted messages collection and view index expiration, are all examples of the work a server can do asynchronously on behalf of users, whether or not they are currently connected to the server.

In general, the load on the server due to background actions such as user-initiated actions, is proportional to the number of users on the server. However, other factors such as whether the server acts as an intersite connector for messages on other servers or hosts a messaging gateway, can have a large impact. On Microsoft Exchange Server computers that act purely as gateways or backbone computers and do not directly host any users, the load due to user-initiated actions is essentially non-existent. In such cases, the load on the server is considered only as a background action.

Inequality of Actions

Although it is often convenient for modeling purposes to think of every user-initiated or background action as being equivalent to every other in terms of the load that each places upon the server, this is not the case. For example, when a 500K message is copied to a user's personal information store, that action places more load on the server than if a 1K message were copied. Similarly, sending a message to a distribution list containing 100 members creates more background actions than sending the message to a single recipient.

You can make accurate predictions about how user-initiated actions will impact the server load if you base your predictions on aggregates over time. For example, if you review the set of actions a user performs during a certain time period, such as an 8-hour work day, you can sum up the user-initiated actions during that time period. You can also quantify some definitions of users by characterizing how many actions they perform per unit time, the set of actions and the individual action's load characteristics (such as estimating the size of messages) and arrive with sample user definitions that can be used for making rough performance predictions of actual user communities.

As an example, you can classify your users as having low, medium, and heavy usage.

A low-usage user could be someone who, on a daily average:

- Sends three messages
- Reads new mail five times and old mail 12 times
- Makes one change to his or her schedule

A medium-usage user, on a daily average:

- Sends six messages
- Reads new mail 15 times and old mail 12 times
- Makes five changes to his or her schedule

A heavy-usage user, on a daily average:

- Sends eight messages
- Reads new mail 20 times and old mail 12 times
- Makes 10 changes to his or her schedule

Types of Users

As mentioned above, traffic and interaction patterns vary greatly. Some organizations rely heavily on their messaging system, which creates very heavy user interaction. Other organizations may not rely so heavily on the messaging system and therefore have low usage levels. The demand your users place on Microsoft Exchange Server has a direct impact on performance and the number of users that can be hosted on one computer. The same hardware, performing the same functionality, can host 500 light users in one organization, but only 150 heavy users in another organization.

Server Load

A server computer consists of the following three hardware elements: one or more CPUs of a given architecture and processing speed, an amount of primary memory (RAM), and one or more disk drives of specific speeds and sizes and their controllers. These hardware elements comprise the critical hardware resources on the server.

When Microsoft Exchange Server services a user-initiated action or performs background actions, it uses each of these resources to some degree over a period of time to perform its operations. For example, responding to an open message request from a client can require several milliseconds of CPU processing time, one or more disk accesses, and enough memory to hold the code and data necessary to perform the operation. In the case where actions occur over a period of time, all of the server hardware is dedicated to each action. Each action is completed as quickly as possible and does not need to wait for hardware resources to become available. In such cases, the Microsoft Exchange Server computer is essentially idle between each action, and the actions are separated sufficiently in time so that they do not overlap. In other words, the server is *unloaded*.

On the other hand, when many users are initiating actions close together in time or a large number of background events are occurring, there is competition for the server hardware resources. Bottlenecks occur when the code servicing a particular action must wait for hardware to become available to complete its tasks. When this happens, the server is said to be *under load*.

Load and Response Time

When a server is under load, actions can take longer to complete than they would if the server were unloaded. For user-initiated actions, this can increase response time. If the server is excessively loaded, users can perceive the server as slow or unresponsive. Imagine a server with specific hardware and a homogenous user community where each user performs the same set of actions randomly but, on average, evenly spaced over a given time interval. With only a single user connected to the server, each user-initiated action is completed before the next is initiated. The response times that user experiences are near the theoretical minimums allowed by the hardware in use on the client and server computers and the underlying network.

However, if you allow more users to connect to the server, actions overlap in time. Microsoft Exchange Server becomes bottlenecked for short durations while one portion of the software performing an action waits for another to relinquish hardware resources. Eventually, this delays actions to the point that user-initiated actions are taking noticeably longer to complete.

This relationship between load and response time defines the number of users any given server can support. At some point, as the load on a server increases, the response times a user experiences move from being acceptable to being unacceptable. This crossover point defines the number of the theoretical, homogenous users that a server's hardware can support.

An Average Workday's Effect on the Server

Actions that cause load are not evenly distributed over time. The morning hours of the workday can exhibit the highest load, when users arrive at work and spend time catching up on e-mail or public folder information that has been generated since the previous day. Conversely, lunch time can represent a lull in the day's activity, as well as evenings and weekends.

Given the number of users Microsoft Exchange Server can typically host, even on smaller server computers, the impulse loads should not represent a large percentage of the total user population on the server except in extreme situations.

Factors Affecting Performance

The type and number of CPUs attached to a Microsoft Exchange Server computer dictate the performance potential for the Microsoft Exchange Server environment. For example, computers based on the Pentium processor offer better performance than computers based on the 486 chip. Also, a 133MHz Pentium performs better than a 100MHz Pentium.

Paging can be viewed as a contention for memory. As with most resources, some contention is tolerable. However, as the contention increases, the system eventually reaches a point where system resources (such as CPU time, bus bandwidth, disk time, and so on) are increasingly passing pages back and forth among the various processes contending for memory. If you were to graph memory contention versus average response times, you would see a smooth line from zero contention up to a point where response times start to increase dramatically. This is often called *thrashing*. As memory contention increases past the point of thrashing, response times typically increase exponentially. Short periods of thrashing can be acceptable for some environments, but you should try to prevent systems from thrashing, especially during active, mission-critical activities.

I/O Subsystem

When examining the input/output (I/O) subsystem as it relates to performance, there are many factors to consider, such as the type and number of disk controllers, the type of drives installed, and the choices required for fault tolerance. Overall system performance on a Microsoft Exchange Server computer can be dramatically affected by these variables.

It is important to use all available small computer system interface (SCSI) channels and to add more channels, if necessary, to improve performance. Also, the addition of more disk drives can help performance. By adding more drives, you can ensure that the workload is distributed more efficiently.

Network Hardware

For optimal network performance, consider adapter types and the type of network medium, such as twisted-pair wire, optical fiber, coaxial cable, and so on. To optimize performance you can: install a high-performance network adapter card in the server; use protocols that are necessary and keep them to a minimum; use multiple network cards; and segment the LAN, if appropriate. Network adapters can provide varying levels of performance. The characteristics of an adapter that can most affect performance involve the bus type, bus width, and the amount of onboard memory on the adapter.

Microsoft Exchange Factors Affecting Usage

When determining the number of users to allow on a Microsoft Exchange Server computer, consider how many users will be connected simultaneously. You might be able to put more user accounts on one server if you know that not all of them will be connected at the same time. For example, if your organization has two shifts of workers, where both sets of users won't be connected to the server at the same time, then more user accounts can be hosted on the same server.

Although a background cost exists when you have more users on a server than are actually connected, it isn't nearly as high as the cost of having more simultaneously connected users.

In summary, the most important comparison to consider is that of background tasks versus user-initiated tasks. Even when a user is not connected, directories will be updated, rules triggered, messages delivered, and other operations will take place on an ongoing basis.

Location and Use of Stores

Microsoft Exchange enables users to store messages in the server-based store or in personal folder (.pst) files on their local computers or on a network drive. Even if a user has personal folders, he or she will also still have a server-based store. In fact, it is not possible for a user to only have personal folder files. The server-based store must exist to receive messages, process rules, and so on. However, if users set their personal folder files as the default delivery location, a lot of work is offloaded from the server. Messages are delivered to the user's server store and rules are triggered on behalf of that user, but these rules can be deferred until the user logs on, if it involves working with the user's .pst file.

Whenever a user requests data from a personal folder, the server does not read the attributes and data into the buffer cache. Instead, all of the processing occurs on the client, because that is where the data is located. In this case, the server does not have to be involved at all. If a user saves a copy of everything in the Sent Mail folder, that process is performed locally. Also, when a user deletes a message, a copy is saved in the local Deleted Items folder and again, the server is not involved.

Public Folder Use and Replication

Using public folders on a Microsoft Exchange Server computer can have a dramatic effect on the server's performance. Size, frequency of user access, various views on that folder, the number of replicas, the replication schedule, and how often its content changes are all factors that affect server performance. If many users access a public folder frequently, then the server is going to be kept busy satisfying those requests. Also, the public folder keeps track of the expansion state of each folder and the read/unread state of each message on a per-user basis.

Although public folder replication is a fast process, changes to a public folder are replicated according to the replication schedule set up by the administrator. Even if the replication schedule is set to **Always**, replication only occurs every 15 minutes. This affects the user because if replication starts when a user is accessing a public folder or the public folder hierarchy, the user will notice a sudden slowdown that improves only when the replication process is completed. If there are a number of public folder replicas to update, then this activity can place even more stress on the server and extend the replication process.

Public folders can contain messages and free-standing documents. Messages are like any other mail message as far as the resources they consume on a server. Free- standing documents, however, raise another issue for performance because they are typically large.

If you post a 1-MB file in a public folder, then any user that accesses that document brings 1 MB of data across the wire. This affects the performance of the server for every user.

Rules and Views

Rules are user-defined actions that require a server to perform on behalf of the user. Typical examples of rules are: displaying a notification when a message is received from a specific person, or automatically moving messages into a specific folder based on the content of the message. Typically, rules have very little effect on overall server performance until most users have more than 10 rules set up.

For views, the server must store and keep track of the indexes that make up a view. Although a cache is used to store the most recently used indexes, a user might notice a small performance hit when opening a seldom-used view.

Microsoft Schedule+

Schedule+ uses a hidden public folder to replicate free/busy information. Within a site, this replication occurs automatically. Between multiple sites, this replication must be set up by the administrator.

The main performance consideration for an administrator working with Schedule+ is whether the user is working with a local schedule file or a server schedule file. If a local file is used, Schedule+ is very responsive and periodically updates the schedule information on the server. However, if a user chooses not to work with a local schedule file, then each change to that schedule causes interaction with the server. Initial testing has shown that not working with a local schedule file causes a significant impact on the users, and if enough users are working in this manner, then it has a negative performance impact on all users.

Connectors and Gateways

Connectors and *gateways* are processes that run on the server. They both contend with Microsoft Exchange processes for resources on the server. These connectors and gateways communicate directly with the information store, which also creates contention for resources.

If a particular connector or gateway is causing performance problems, you can dedicate a computer to this connector or gateway, or add a second connector or gateway instance somewhere else in the site.

Directories, Replication, and the Bridgehead Server

A *bridgehead server* acts as the door in and out of the site's directory. When you configure a directory replication connector between two sites, you can choose which server in each site will act as the bridgehead server. It is the responsibility of this bridgehead server to exchange all directory updates with the partner bridgehead server. Within a site, directory replication occurs among all servers. Because this processing is proportional to the number of directory changes that occur, it is difficult to predict how it will affect the overall performance of a server. During a migration to Microsoft Exchange Server, when the directory is changing often, or in organizations where hundreds of directory updates occur every day, the directory replication process can negatively impact performance.

Message Transfer Agent

The main responsibility of the message transfer agent (MTA) is to route messages between multiple servers. Even in a single-server scenario, the MTA also has tasks to perform, including the expansion of distribution lists and the routing of outgoing gateway or connector messages. The MTA has the greatest impact on performance when multiple Microsoft Exchange Server computers are deployed.

Network Quality and Connectivity

If you place a Microsoft Exchange Server computer on a Fiber Distributed Data Interface (FDDI) ring with a 100-MB capacity, that server will provide better connectivity and performance than a server attached to a token-ring network. An overloaded Ethernet segment with many collisions occurring will also reduce the performance of the server. Wide area network (WAN) connectivity and quality should also be considered, especially if you are trying to determine site boundaries or whether to have clients access their server across the WAN.

Determining Server Limits

There is no explicit limit on the number of users you can configure to reside on a single Microsoft Exchange Server computer. However, there can be practical limitations dictated by the time it takes to back up a very large server database. Practical limits not directly related to server performance can prove to be the limiting factor on the number of users a server can support.

There is a 16-GB limitation on the size of the public and private information store databases (32 GB total), but this limitation will be removed in the next version of Microsoft Exchange Server. Presently, this limitation can become a factor on larger servers hosting many users, depending on the following factors:

- The amount of server storage used by each client.
- Whether client quota limitations are used and their values.
- The degree to which single-instancing of messages and attachments increases the logical storage capacity of the server.
- The extent to which personal folders are used, and to a lesser extent, the number of rules, views, and finders that are defined by users on the server.

Testing Methodology

To testing your methodology when determining the number of users supported by a server, you should follow the four steps below:

1. Optimize your server. Optimization includes optimizing the hardware and Microsoft Exchange Server Setup.
2. Classify your users and set expectations as to what acceptable response times they will need.
3. Calculate your user data and use the Load Simulator tool.
4. Analyze your data.

Step One: Optimizing Your Server

This section describes how to configure the hardware you are using with Microsoft Exchange Server.

Configuring Your CPU

There is not a lot you can do to optimize your CPU. However, it is important to note that Microsoft Exchange Server does not scale well past four CPUs. For example, a Windows NT® Server computer dedicated to a Microsoft Exchange Server organization with more than four CPUs does not provide a boost in performance. Those CPUs could be put to better use elsewhere. As far as the type of CPU is concerned, the faster the better. Therefore, using a Pentium 133 chip provides much more performance than a 486/66 and a little more performance than a Pentium 100.

There is one optimization step you can take with Windows NT Server that improves how your server uses its CPUs.

▶ **To optimize how your server uses its CPUs**

1. In Control Panel, double-click the **System** icon.

2. Choose the **Performance** tab.

3. Under application performance, boost the slider bar to halfway between **None** and **Maximum**.

This boosts the system priorities that Windows NT Server places on background tasks.

Using Memory

Microsoft Exchange Server uses all the memory you can give it, up to the total size of your information store. At that point, your entire database is in memory. The minimum amount of random access memory (RAM) recommended for Microsoft Exchange Server is 24 MB, but testing has shown that having 64 to 128 MB of RAM provides much better performance than an upgraded CPU.

▶ **To maximize the memory usage of your Windows NT Server computer**

1. In Control Panel, double-click the Network icon.

2. Select the Services tab, then select Server.

3. Select Properties, then select Maximize Throughput for Network Applications.

You can also configure virtual memory to use a larger page file. It is difficult to determine exactly how large the page file should be, but a good rule of thumb is to choose 125 MB plus the amount of physical RAM. For example, if your server has 64 MB of RAM, you can set the page file size to 189 MB (125 plus 64).

Disk I/O Subsystem

The Disk I/O subsystem is one area where much optimization can be accomplished. However, before you try to optimize the disk I/O subsystem in your computer, you should understand the following background information.

Server Transaction Logs

Microsoft Exchange Server issues I/Os to the disk subsystem on the server to read data from disk into memory or to write data out to permanent storage. For example, when a user opens his or her Inbox, the set of properties in the default folder view must be accessed for each of the first 20 messages in the Inbox folder and returned to the user. If this information is not cached in memory on the server from a recent access, it must be read from the server information store database on disk before the action is completed. The disk read I/O is synchronous to the user-initiated action.

Similarly, if a message is transferred from another server, the message must be secured to disk before the receipt of the message can be acknowledged. This prevents message loss in case of power outages.

The disk I/Os issued by Microsoft Exchange Server are either reads or writes and are either synchronous or asynchronous. Additionally, while all read I/Os and asynchronous write I/Os may be considered random, many of the synchronous writes issued by Microsoft Exchange Server are sequential. That is, a special method of writing changes to disk known as a sequential, write-ahead transaction log is used to speed up actions that require synchronous write I/O.

If the I/O to the drive is completely sequential in nature, the disk head generally does not move at all and only occasionally needs to shift over a single track. The average seek drops close to zero, dramatically increasing the number of disk I/Os per second that the drive can support.

For this reason, hosting Microsoft Exchange Server database transaction logs on a dedicated physical disk drive is critical in ensuring good disk write I/O performance. Placing the information store transaction logs on a physical disk with no other sources of disk I/O on the drive is the single most important aspect of improving Microsoft Exchange Server performance.

It is best to use the file allocation table (FAT) file system for this drive because it performs the best with sequential activity. However, note that the Windows NT file system (NTFS) must be used after this log exceeds 2 GB.

Random Disk Access I/O

Other than the transaction logs, the remaining sources of disk I/O on Microsoft Exchange Server are generally random in nature. This includes the Windows NT page file, server databases, message tracking logs, and so on. The number of disk I/Os issued by the different parts of the system will vary over time while different server components do their work. For example, when a message is received from another server and delivered to a user, the MTA first secures the message to disk in its transient database, which causes a single random write to the MTADATA directory. It then makes a call to the system attendant, which writes a log entry into the message tracking log. Finally, the MTA then notifies the information store that a message is available, at which time the information store receives a message from the MTA and writes the message into a permanent database. This generates synchronous write I/O to the information store transaction log, and asynchronous read and write I/O to the information store database in the MDBDATA directory.

Because the source of these random server disk I/Os varies, you can combine the remaining disk drives into a software or hardware stripe-set, which enables the combined capacity of all the remaining disk drives in the system to be made available to any server component that is performing I/O.

Using a Page File

You use a page file when the processes running on a Windows NT computer (including Windows NT itself) need more code and/or data pages over a period of time than there is physical memory in the computer.

If you have a lower-memory Microsoft Exchange Server computer, (for example, a computer with 24 MB and 50 to 100 users), some paging will occur on computers completing the normal set of Microsoft Exchange Server processes, such as handling user requests, moving mail off or onto a server, and so on.

Paging makes up a significant percentage of your total disk I/O because the working sets of all the Microsoft Exchange Server (and Windows NT Server) processes don't completely fit in physical memory all at once. Paging is a technique for implementing virtual memory. If the server is the only one in the site and off-server traffic is minimal, the MTA won't be doing much (except for expanding the occasional distribution list) and it will leave more room for the rest of the server processes, which results in less paging. Conversely, more paging will occur if you run additional processes on the same computer (beyond the core Microsoft Exchange Server services such as the Internet Mail Service), or if you import directory objects, generate the Offline Address Book, start up the server services, or do anything else that is non-typical.

If you have enough memory in your Microsoft Exchange Server computer such that the majority of the pages needed by all server processes fit into physical memory at the same time, you won't page very much during normal operation. Remember, however, that the working set of the information store and the directory store includes the buffer caches. Even on larger computers with 128 MB or more of RAM, you can page with very little activity if the buffer caches are set too high for the amount of RAM in the computer.

It is not recommended to dedicate a disk just to the page file because if you are paging, you will achieve better I/O performance by combining that drive into the stripe set and placing the page file there. If you aren't paging, it wastes drive space. It's best to stripe drives together to handle large databases because they are large, single files. You probably won't have many separate partitions over which to spread the page file, so placing it on the stripe set achieves the same result.

Running the Performance Optimizer

A server under load that exhibits poor response time will generally be bottlenecked on one or more of the three critical server hardware resources: CPU processing capacity, RAM, or the I/O subsystem.

Servers vary widely from low-end single processor, single-disk servers with small amounts of RAM to giant multiprocessor computers that rival the power of mainframes. Microsoft Exchange Server will run on all of them, but there are configuration settings that need to be adjusted to ensure that Microsoft Exchange Server is properly optimized for your specific server hardware.

The Microsoft Exchange Performance Optimizer automatically detects your server's hardware and adjusts configuration settings that are hardware-dependent. If you have not run the Optimizer after installing Microsoft Exchange Server on your server hardware, it will most likely perform poorly. Any time you add or remove hardware to your Microsoft Exchange Server computer, you should rerun the Optimizer to ensure that Microsoft Exchange Server is properly tuned for your hardware.

Using Load Simulator

If you are trying to determine the optimum number of users per server on your own, it is important to represent the users as accurately as possible. Some organizations have no idea how their user base will use Microsoft Exchange Server because they may have never had any messaging products on which to base their numbers. Other organizations will have some idea, based on previous experience, as to how their users will use a messaging platform. However, Microsoft Exchange Server may provide features and functionality that have never been available to their user community, so the organization may not fully understand what impact these new features can have.

For testing purposes, users are classified as having low, medium, and heavy usage. Initially, the users' states were as follows:

Parameter	Low-Usage User	Medium-Usage User	Heavy-Usage User
Number of non-default folders	20	40	60
Number of messages per folder	5	5	5
Number of messages in Inbox	1	4	9
Number of messages in Deleted Items folder	1	1	1

For testing purposes, we defined low-usage users as those who do the following on a daily basis:

- Divide their time into an 8-hour daytime and a 4-hour nighttime.

- Originate three new messages (that is, not replies and forwards) to four recipients, and save a copy of these messages in the Sent Mail folder.

- Read new mail five times and old mail 12 times.

Note   Reading new mail consists of opening the Inbox and reading every piece of new mail that the user has received. Reading old mail consists of selecting one folder at random and reading one message in that folder.

Testing demonstrated that light users:

- Used the following commands when working with messages: **Reply** (10 percent of the time), **Reply All** (3 percent), **Forward** (5 percent), **Move** (none of the time), **Copy** (one of the time), and **Delete** (40 percent).

- Loaded 25 percent of the attachments received.

- Limited their Inbox to 20 messages.

- Emptied their Deleted Items folder once.

- Made one change to their schedule.

Medium-usage users were defined as those who do the following on a daily basis:

- Divide their day into an 8-hour daytime and a 4-hour nighttime.
- Compose six new messages (that is, not replies and forwards) to four recipients, saving a copy of them in the Sent Mail folder.
- Read new mail 15 times and old mail 12 times.

Testing demonstrated that medium users:

- Used the following commands when working with messages: **Reply** (15 percent of the time), **Reply All** (5 percent), **Forward** (7 percent), **Move** (20 percent), **Copy** (none of the time), and **Delete** (40 percent).
- Loaded 25 percent of the attachments they received.
- Limited their Inbox to 125 messages.
- Emptied their Deleted Items folder once.
- Made five changes to their schedule.

Heavy-usage users were defined as those who do the following on a daily basis:

- Divide their time into an 8-hour daytime and a 4-hour nighttime.
- Originate eight new messages (that is, not replies and forwards) to five recipients, saving a copy of them in the Sent Mail folder.
- Read new mail 20 times and old mail 12 times.

Testing demonstrated that heavy users:

- Used the following commands when working with messages: **Reply** (20 percent), **Reply All** (7 percent), **Forward** (7 percent), **Move** (20 percent), **Copy** (none of the time), and **Delete** (40 percent).
- Loaded 25% of the attachments received
- Limited their Inbox to 250 messages.
- Emptied their Deleted Items folder once.
- Made 10 changes to their schedule.

The data above generated the following computed averages:

	Light User	**Medium User**	**Heavy User**
Messages sent per day	6.7	19.8	38.6
Messages received per day	20.4	55.9	118.9

The message mix for these users was also varied. Four different message types/sizes were used: 1K, 2K, and 4K messages, plus a message with a 10K attachment. A mix of these messages was used for each user type and weighted as follows:

Message Size/Type	Light User	Medium User	Heavy User
1K message	9	7	6
2K message	(none)	2	2
4K message	(none)	(none)	1
10K attachment	1	1	1

Server Definitions

The following table lists the criteria used to define low-end, middle, and high-end servers:

Server Type	Manufacturer	Processor	RAM	Disk Config	Network
Low-End					
Server A	Gateway 2000	1- 486/66	32 MB	1 - 515MB 1 - 1 GB	Intel EtherExpress Pro
Server B	Compaq Proliant	1 - 486/66	32 MB	1 - 1 GB 1 - 2 GB	Compaq Netflex II
Middle					
Server C	Compaq Proliant	2 - 486/66	64 MB	1 - 2 GB	Compaq Netflex II
Server D	Compaq Proliant	1 - Pentium 90	64 MB	1 - 2 GB 1 - 8 GB Stripe	Compaq Netflex II
High-End					
Server E	AT&T 3555	8 - Pentium 90	512 MB	2 - 2 GB 1 - 24 GB Stripe 1 - 16 GB	3COM Etherlink III

Running Load Simulator

Following are the basic steps for running Load Simulator.

▶ **To run Load Simulator**

1. Verify that you have classified your users and set up the servers you want to test.

2. Install the Microsoft Exchange Client on the Windows NT Workstation computers or Windows NT Server computers you plan to use as the Load Simulator clients. (Note that Load Simulator only runs under Windows NT.)

3. Determine what the acceptable response time should be for your users. Usually, 1 second (1000 milliseconds) is a good criteria to use, but you may decide that 1.5 seconds (1500 milliseconds) is adequate.

4. Using Load Simulator, define your test topology and generate your user import files.

5. For each server you plan to test, use the Microsoft Exchange Server Administrator program to import those user definitions into your Microsoft Exchange Server directory.

6. Using Load Simulator, define the initial state of both your users and public folders.

7. Run the User Initialization and Public Folder Initialization tests against your server to populate the Microsoft Exchange Server information store.

8. Define a few tests with the user classifications that you have previously defined and run them against the server platforms. For example, you may decide you want to test 250 light users against a middle-defined server.

9. Each pass of Load Simulator tool runs for several hours and produces one number that is the 95-percent weighted average response time (in milliseconds) that each of the Load Simulator users experienced during that test. You can use several different user counts to generate several different data points and then graph the results.

Detecting Performance Bottlenecks

If you have a user who complains that the server is running too slowly, do you need to buy more hardware? It is important to realize that detecting performance bottlenecks is an art and that your ability to do so will improve with experience. For example, you may think that memory is your bottleneck. However, if you purchase more memory for your server, you may discover that the server still isn't performing better because the CPU is the bottleneck.

The goal is to determine which of the three major parts of the server—memory, disk I/O subsystem, or CPU—is causing the bottleneck. The Windows NT Performance Monitor tool can be an effective aid in making the correct decision.

Memory

To determine if the system requires more memory, you need to find out how much your system is paging. Use the Performance Monitor to track the following elements of the paging file: percentage usage and memory percent available. If the paging file is more than 50 percent used and if less than 25 percent of the total memory is available, then it's best to add more RAM.

Disk I/O

To determine whether the disk I/O subsystem is the bottleneck, you need to find out if the server is being I/O-bound on asynchronous I/Os to the Microsoft Exchange Server database. To determine this, review the following performance monitor counters: PhysicalDisk: Disk Queue Length and PhysicalDisk: %Disk Time.

The Disk Queue Length parameter shows how many outstanding disk requests there are per physical disk. It includes requests in service at that time. Multi-spindle disk devices can have multiple disk requests active at one time. Therefore, look for the disk queue length minus the number of spindles on the disk device. The disk is I/O-bound when the difference between the length of the queue and the number of spindles on the disk device is consistently high. According to the Windows NT Performance Monitor, this difference should average less than two.

Disk time is the percentage of elapsed time that the selected disk drive spends servicing requests. A high percentage indicates that your system is spending most of its time servicing disk requests. In this case, your system needs either faster disk drives or more disk drives over which to spread the requests.

CPU

The CPU can have a high utilization even if the disk and/or memory are causing the bottleneck. Therefore, it's best to check those two areas before checking the CPU. To determine if your system requires more processors, track System: % Total Processor and Process: % Processor - Process X. If the total system processor use is averaging more than 75 percent, you probably need to add another processor. So if you already have four CPUs and are still CPU-bound, you need to upgrade the processor type or add a second server.

Conclusion

How many users can you host on a single Microsoft Exchange Server computer?

As has been shown, this question is not simple to answer. Even the question itself must be defined before you can proceed. To answer this question, you must first define what a user or a server actually means. It is also important to remember that different organizations will generate different results that are specific to their environment.

By knowing what factors affect Microsoft Exchange Server performance, how to optimize your configuration, and what to look for when trying to detect bottlenecks, you can maintain a more efficient Microsoft Exchange Server organization.

The following section describes the different processes developed to automate the setup of Microsoft Exchange Server and Microsoft Exchange Client. Each section has a set of prerequisites as well as a defined process showing you how to complete the installation.

Updating Windows NT Server 3.51 to Service Pack 4

Windows NT Server 3.51 must already be installed on the server computer, and all users must be logged off of Windows NT Server before you update Windows NT Server 3.51 to Service Pack 4.

Procedure

Use the following procedure to update Windows NT Server version 3.51 to Service Pack 4.

▶ **To update Windows NT Server 3.51 to Service Pack 4**

- Using the built-in scheduling service in Windows NT Server, schedule the Ntsp4upd.bat file to run when no users are logged on to the server (some time at night is usually best). This batch file takes one argument—the name of the server where the installation directory resides (and from which the Windows NT Server 3.51 Service Pack 4 will be installed). An example of a typical argument might be **ntsp4upd cisvr002**.

  Note that the batch file uses drive X, so any previous connections made to this drive will be disconnected during the setup process.

This batch file will apply the Service Pack unattended and reboot the server.

Setup Options

After you have updated Windows NT 3.51 to Service Pack 4, you can choose from the following three possibilities to set up a new Microsoft Exchange Server computer.

- A Microsoft Exchange Server computer that will create a new site. The batch file for this setup is Newsite.bat.

- A Microsoft Exchange Server computer that will join an existing site, for example, a new server in an existing Microsoft Exchange site. The batch file for this setup is Newsrv.bat

- An administrative-only computer. The batch file for this setup is Newadmin.bat. This type of setup needs to be completed for any server intended to back up Microsoft Exchange Server, and for any server that will be used as a Microsoft Exchange Server administrator console. To run this setup, you need to schedule the correct .bat file to run in the Windows NT Server scheduler.

Updating Microsoft Exchange Server 4.0 to Microsoft Exchange Server Service Pack 1

Microsoft Exchange Server 4.0 must already be installed on the server computer, and all Microsoft Exchange users must be logged off of Microsoft Exchange Server before you update Windows NT Server 4.0 to Service Pack 1.

Procedure

Use the following procedure to update Microsoft Exchange Server 4.0 to Service Pack 1.

▶ **To update Microsoft Exchange Server to Service Pack 1**

- Using the built-in scheduling service in Windows NT Server, schedule the Exsp1upd.bat file to run when no users are logged on to the server (some time overnight is usually best). This batch file takes one argument—the name of the server where the installation directory resides (and from which Microsoft Exchange Server 4.0 Service Pack 1 will be installed). An example of a typical argument might be **exsp1upd cisvr002**.

  Note that the batch file uses drive X, so any previous connections made to this drive will be disconnected during the setup process.

This batch file will stop all of the Microsoft Exchange Server services, apply Service Pack 1 unattended, and then restart all of the services.

Optimizing Microsoft Exchange Server Performance

Microsoft Exchange Server 4.0 must already be installed on the server computer. All Microsoft Exchange users must be logged off of Microsoft Exchange Server before this process starts.

Running the Performance Optimizer

This process has not been automated. Therefore, to complete this process, you must be logged on to the Windows NT Server computer where Microsoft Exchange Server is installed. To optimize performance, run the Microsoft Exchange Server Performance Optimizer (located in the Microsoft Exchange program group). The Performance Optimizer will stop all Microsoft Exchange Server services, and then prompt you for the following information:

How many users will this server host?

This should be the number of users located in that office.

What services will run on this server?

Select all options (Private Mailbox, Public Folders, Connector, and Multi-server. The services that should be chosen depend on the organization.

How many users will be in the entire Microsoft Exchange Server organization?

The recommended number of users is between 1,000 and 9,999 (depending on the organization).

How much memory should Microsoft Exchange Server use?

It is recommended that this remain at zero, which means that Microsoft Exchange will use all available memory. Note that this ultimately depends on the organization, as an organization might run another process on the same server.

After answering these questions, perform the following steps:

1. Choose **Next**. A window is displayed indicating that the program will run tests on the disk partitions.

2. After the tests are completed, choose **Next**. Performance Optimizer displays a window that indicates the optimal locations for the various Microsoft Exchange Server databases and transaction logs.

3. Choose **Next** to accept the defaults.

4. To move the file automatically, choose **Next**.

5. When the display prompts you to restart the Microsoft Exchange Server services, choose **Finish**.

Automated Installation of Microsoft Exchange Client

The following are procedures for installing Microsoft Exchange Client on a Windows NT workstation.

Procedure

Because Microsoft Systems Management Server (SMS) is not fully deployed at this time, it cannot be used to deploy the Microsoft Exchange Client. However, there is a simple command you can run to complete an automated installation.

▶ **To complete an automated installation of Microsoft Exchange Client**

1. Because users cannot install this software on their local computers, you must log on to a workstation.

2. After you log on to the workstation, run the **Instexch.bat** file. This batch file takes one argument—the name of the server where the installation directory resides (and from which Microsoft Exchange Client 4.0 will be installed). An example of a typical argument might be **instexch cisvr002**.

3. Note that the batch file uses drive X, so any previous connections made to this drive will be disconnected during the setup process.

This batch file will set up the necessary Microsoft Exchange Client software onto the workstation without any interaction from the Administrator.

Creating User Profiles

Note that Microsoft Exchange Client 4.0 must already be installed on the client before you create the user profile. Also, you must run this process for every user who logs on to the workstation and wants to access his or her mail.

▶ **To create a user profile**

1. Log on to a workstation as the user.

2. Run the **Doprof.bat** file. This batch file takes one argument—the name of the server where the installation directory resides (and from which the Microsoft Exchange Client 4.0 will be installed). An example of a typical argument might be **doprof cisvr002**.

   Note that the batch file uses drive X, so any previous connections made to this drive will be disconnected during the setup process.

This batch file will create a Microsoft Exchange Client profile for the currently logged-on user.

C H A P T E R   2

Working with Microsoft Exchange Server

The following sections in this chapter can help you gain more flexibility when working with Microsoft Exchange Server:

- Using Russian, Eastern European, Greek, and Turkish Language Character Sets
- Message Transfer Agent (MTA) Routing
- Fan-out
- Moving Microsoft Exchange Server to Another Computer

Using Russian, Eastern European, Greek, and Turkish Language Character Sets

This section describes the steps needed to use the Microsoft Exchange Internet Mail Service with Russian and Eastern European character sets.

Russian and Eastern European Character Sets

Use the procedures below to work with Russian and Eastern European language character sets.

Setup

Before making any changes to the Microsoft Exchange Internet Mail Service, make sure that C_1250.nls (Eastern European Latin2) or C_1251.nls (Russian) is in your \<*Windows NT Root*>\System32 directory, and that the following is added to the system registry:

HKEY_LOCAL_MACHINE\System\CurrentControlSet\Control \NLSCodepage

    1250 = REG_SZ "c_1250.nls" (Latin2)

    1251 = REG_SZ "c_1251.nls" (Russian)

Installation

Use the following procedures to install Russian or Eastern European character sets.

▶ **To install Russian or Eastern European character sets**

- If you want to install the Russian character set, copy the KOI8-R.trn file from the localized client software to the \Exchsrvr\Connect\Trn directory on your Microsoft Exchange Server computer;

  –or–

  If you want to install the Polish, Czech, or Hungarian character set, copy the ISO88592.trn file from the localized client software to the \Exchsrvr\Connect\Trn directory on your Microsoft Exchange Server computer.

Adding Russian or Eastern European Character Sets as a Global Option

- To add the Russian character set as a global option, start the Microsoft Exchange Administrator program and set the "Internet Mail Character Set Translation" MIME and non-MIME to KOI8-R when using the Russian character set.

- To add the Polish, Czech or Hungarian character sets as global options, set the "Internet Mail Character Set Translation" MIME and non-MIME to ISO 8859-2.

Specifying Message Content by E-mail Domain

If you do not want to set Russian or Eastern European character sets as global options, the message content can be specified by e-mail domain.

▶ **To specify message content by e-mail domain**

1. In the Microsoft Exchange Server Administrator program, select a server, and then select **Configuration**.
2. Choose **Connections**, and then select **Internet Mail Service**.
3. Select the **Internet Mail** tab, and then choose **E-Mail Domain**.
4. Select a character set.

Changing the Windows NT Registry to Use the Russian Character Set

To use the Russian character set, open the Windows NT Registry Editor and add the following information:

HKEY_CLASSES_ROOT\MIME\Database

> **Charset**

> **koi8-r**

>> **Codepage = REG_DWORD 0x04E3 (1251)**

Codepage

> **1251**

>> **BodyCharset = REG_SZ "koi8-r"**

Changing the Windows NT Registry to Use the Polish, Czech, or Hungarian Character Set

To use the Polish, Czech, or Hungarian character set, add these entries to the Windows NT registry:

HKEY_CLASSES_ROOT\MIME\Database

> **Charset**

> **iso-8859-2**

>> **Codepage = REG_DWORD 0x04e2 (1250)**

Codepage

> **1250**

>> **BodyCharset = REG_SZ "iso-8859-2"**

To ensure that the character sets take effect, you must restart the Microsoft Exchange Internet Mail Service after making changes to Microsoft Exchange Server or the Windows NT registry.

Greek and Turkish Character Sets

If you want to use Greek or Turkish character sets with the Microsoft Exchange Server Internet Mail Service, follow the steps in the sections below before viewing one of these languages.

Note Before making any changes to the Microsoft Exchange Server Internet Mail Service, make sure that these file names are available in your Windows NT\System32 directory: C_1253.nls (Greek) or C_1254.nls (Turkish). Then make sure that the following entries are added to your system registry:

**HKEY_LOCAL_MACHINE\
System\CurrentControlSet\Control\NLSCodepage**

      1250 = REG_SZ "c_1253.nls" (Greek)

      1251 = REG_SZ "c_1254.nls" (Turkish)

Installation

Use the following procedure to install Greek and Turkish character sets.

▶ **To install Greek and Turkish character sets**

- To install Greek character sets, from your Windows NT Service Pack 3 compact disc, copy the ISO88597.trn file to the \Exchsrvr\Connect\Trn directory on your Microsoft Exchange Server computer.

- To install Turkish character sets, from your Windows NT Service Pack 3 compact disc, copy the ISO88599.trn file to the \Exchsrvr\Connect\Trn directory on your Microsoft Exchange Server computer.

Adding Greek or Turkish Character Sets as a Global Option

- To use the Greek character set, start the Microsoft Exchange Administrator program and set the "Internet Mail Character Set Translation" MIME and non-MIME to ISO 8859-7.

- To use the Turkish character set, set the "Internet Mail Character Set Translation" MIME and non-MIME to ISO 8859-9.

Specifying Message Content by E-mail Domain

If you do not want to set Greek or Turkish character sets as global options, the message content can be specified by e-mail domain.

1. In the Microsoft Exchange Server Administrator program, select a server, and then select **Configuration**.

2. Choose Connections, and then select Internet Mail Service.

3. Select the **Internet Mail** tab, and then choose **E-Mail Domain**.

4. Select a character set.

Changing the Windows NT Registry to Use the Greek Character Set

To use the Greek character set, open the Windows NT Registry Editor and add the following information:

HKEY_CLASSES_ROOT\MIME\Database

   Charset

   iso-8859-7

      Codepage = REG_DWORD 0x04E5 (1253)

   Codepage

   1253

      BodyCharset = REG_SZ "iso-8859-7"

After adding these entries, restart the Microsoft Exchange Internet Mail Service.

Changing the Windows NT Registry to Use the Turkish Character Set

To use the Turkish character set, add these entries to the Windows NT Registry:

HKEY_CLASSES_ROOT\MIME\Database

   Charset

   iso-8859-9

      Codepage = REG_DWORD 0x04e6 (1254)

   Codepage

   1254

      BodyCharset = REG_SZ "iso-8859-9"

After adding these entries, restart the Microsoft Exchange Internet Mail Service.

Microsoft Exchange Server MTA Routing

The Microsoft Exchange Server MTA can send mail externally to:

- Microsoft Exchange MTAs in the same site, by using remote procedure calls (RPCs).
- Microsoft Exchange MTAs in a different site, through the Site Connector.
- Microsoft Exchange MTAs in a different site, through the Dynamic RAS Connector.
- Remote X.400 MTAs, through an X.400 Connector such as X.25, Transport Control Protocol/Internet Protocol (TCP/IP), or TP4.
- Gateways such as the Microsoft Mail Connector or Internet Mail Service.

Associated with each connector is an address space (or spaces), cost, and possibly a connected site (or sites). These associations are defined by using the Microsoft Exchange Server Administrator program, and are subsequently used to generate the Gateway Routing Table (GWART). An enterprise-wide GWART is created in each site by the Routing Information Daemon (RID), which accesses local information and replicated site GWARTs to build a consolidated local GWART.

A mail message can be either a P1 message, probe, or report. Each responsible recipient of a message is routed individually. Before routing a recipient, the MTA obtains as much address information for the recipient as possible. For more information, see the "Name Resolution" section. If the recipient is local to the current MTA's address space, local routing takes place. If not, remote routing takes place. This process involves routing (through the GWART), selection, and load balancing for each recipient to obtain the routing destination.

Name Resolution

The recipient address (or O/R Name) consists of either the distinguished name (DN) or the X.400 O/R address, or both. The X.400 O/R address is logically divided into standard X.400 O/R address attributes and domain-defined attributes (DDAs). A *one-off routing address* is a manually entered O/R address that is not held in the directory and therefore has no DN. A valid X.400 O/R address is required for routing out of the site, even if only a DDA is specified in a one-off routing address.

Following is the name resolution process:

1. If the recipient address contains no DN, verify whether a DN has been saved within the DDA fields (in an earlier pass through an MTA that constructed an O/R address), and use that if it exists.
2. If a DN exists, read the O/R address for that DN.
3. Perform basic checking on any O/R address.

4. If the original DN was invalid or no DN exists, scan the local proxy addresses to find a match with the O/R address, and then obtain the DN. If the initial scan fails, but a common name or surname exists, perform a "fuzzy match" scan for a unique matching DN.

5. If the current O/R address is invalid, add the local global domain identifier (GDI) to make it valid.

When new address information for a recipient is found, the P1 recipient address is re-encoded into the message. After a message has been routed through the GWART, further name resolution may be required (for more information, see the "Remote Mailboxes" section).

Local Recipients (Mailboxes)

A recipient is considered to be *local* and is not routed through the GWART if a distinguished name for the recipient is available that matches the local site, and the distinguished name does not identify a custom recipient. If a recipient has only an O/R address that matches the local site O/R address space, then a distinguished name will be found by proxy search if the recipient is a valid local recipient. If no distinguished name is found, the recipient will be routed through the GWART.

Address space filtering is performed in the GWART routing routine to ensure that O/R addresses matching the local site O/R address space are not sent out of the site. If a recipient is to be routed through the GWART and matches the local O/R address space, this recipient is marked for non-delivery receipt (NDR). This option can be disabled if you use the Administrator program **Share address space with other local systems** option. To do so, in the Administrator window, choose a recipient, and then select the **General** tab. Choose **Configuration**, and then select **Site Addressing**.

If a local recipient originally had a distinguished name, and an O/R address is found by a proxy search, no re-encode of the P1 recipient address is performed because the O/R address is not required when routing locally. The exception to this is if Recipient_Disclosure is allowed, the O/R address must be included to prevent interoperability problems.

Remote Mailboxes

Any recipients who are not local and also are not DLs or custom recipients are treated as remote mailboxes. Remote mailboxes must always have a valid O/R address (a distinguished name is optional).

A valid O/R address is required to enable X.400 backbones of the message. If a distinguished name is successfully routed through the GWART, and no O/R address is available, a new address is constructed from the remote site proxy O/R address information in the connected sites.

If the new O/R address contains no DDA information, then the distinguished name is saved in the DDA of the O/R address with the special "MSXCHNGE" DDA Type to mark this O/R address as artificially constructed. This mechanism also enables encapsulation of Microsoft Exchange Server distinguished names over 1984 X.400 backbones.

Distribution List Handling

A message containing a distribution list (DL) recipient is first routed to the designated DL expansion point if the DL has a Home-MTA (or locally if none is defined). If the message is routed locally, first a DL-expansion message copy is produced by fan-out, whose recipients are the DL members. This copy is passed back through the routing process. This process is repeated recursively for each nested level of the DL. The MTA verifies that an infinite loop is not generated by DL expansion.

Each MTA can also be configured to not expand replicated remote site DLs (use the **MTA Site Configuration\General** tab in the Administrator program).

Custom Recipients

Custom recipients have a distinguished name that is of local significance only, therefore the distinguished name of a custom recipient is always ignored when routing the recipient through the GWART. The distinguished name and primary X.400 proxy O/R address of a custom recipient are contained in the P1 recipient address, but do not participate in routing. Instead, routing is accomplished through the Target Address attribute of the custom recipient.

Custom recipients have multiple proxy addresses of different types, but only one target address. The target address type typically matches the native mail system used to deliver mail to that custom recipient.

For routing purposes only, X.400 target addresses override the standard O/R address, and non-X.400 target addresses override the DDA portion of the O/R address. If the target address type is not X.400, it is used to route through the DDA arms of the GWART. The target address is not used to overwrite the original recipient address in the P1 of the message. If not originally specified, the target address will be created from the X.400 proxy address found by reading the distinguished name, as with mailboxes.

If no target address is found for the custom recipient, the primary X.400 proxy O/R address (if any) is used for routing.

How the MTA Is Routed

Each recipient of a message is routed individually. The MTA obtains as much address information for the recipient as possible. If the recipient is local to the current MTA's site, local routing is accomplished by using the object's Home-MTA and Home-MDB attributes.

For non-local recipients, the following routing process determines which connector a message is sent through.

- **Route Selection** — Determines *all* of the connectors that can deliver the message.
- **Connector Selection** — Determines the *best* connector to use from the set of available connectors.

Route Selection

The Microsoft Exchange MTA compares the recipient address to the GWART to determine the group of connectors that the message can be delivered to. The search for a match in the GWART is done in the following order:

1. **Distinguished name (DN)** — The native Microsoft Exchange address format. This is only searched if a DN for the recipient has been found. An exact match on the enterprise and site of the DN is required.

2. **Domain-defined attribute (DDA)** — The format in which custom recipient addresses are stored, for example, Microsoft Mail and simple mail transport protocol (SMTP). An exact, wildcard, or partial match on the domain-defined attribute value (DDAV) is required with an exact or partial match on the domain-defined attribute type (DDAT). Wildcard matches are used in order of the exactness of the match (that is, with the exact match first, followed by the wildcard that has the most matching characters, and so on).

3. **O/R address** — Native X.400 address type. An exact or wildcard match on the address space is required. Each field is compared hierarchically with the contents of the GWART for that field until either a match is found or it is determined that no match is present, at which point this recipient is marked for a non-delivery receipt (NDR). The hierarchy is:

   - Country
   - administrative management domain (ADMD)
   - private management domain (PRMD)
   - Organization
   - Organizational Units.

The final result of this search provides a group of connectors that can process the message.

The routing process is called from the following areas:

- Message and probe routing
- Distribution list expansion (route to Home-MTA and detect loops in the DL expansion tree)
- Rerouting (all object types)
- Report routing (normal and DL-specific)

Connector Selection

After a list of suitable connectors has been determined, the MTA needs to determine which connector is the best one to use. This determination is based on the following criteria: the final group of connectors and load balancing.

Connector Grouping

Each connector has a Max Open Retry count and an Open Retry timer configured in the DSA. Site connectors use a site-wide configurable value. If the initial attempt to open an association fails, then a timer of length Open Retry is started for the association control block (ASB) handling the original association. After the timer begins another attempt to open an association, it is processed for that ASB. This process can be repeated Max Open Retry count times for each connector. After the maximum number of retry counts has been used on all available connectors, the message will NDR for the set of recipients for which that connector is to be used. The retry count for each connector is stored on the message in question and updated during rerouting.

1. If the message has not been rerouted in this MTA, exclude the connector that this message came in on, to avoid immediate loop detection.
2. Select the group of connectors where the message retry count is less than the Max Open Retry count for the connector.
3. Activation schedule: X.400 Connectors and Dynamic RAS Connectors follow an *activation schedule* that determines how connections are scheduled to the remote system.

   There are four possible settings for the activation schedule:

   - Active always
   - Selected times (according to the activation schedule)
   - Remote initiated
   - Never active

   Site Connectors, the Internet Mail Service, Microsoft Mail Connectors, and other XAPI gateways are always active.

In addition to the activation schedule, for purposes of routing, there are four activation states. They are, in order of preference:

- Active now
- Will become active
- Remote initiated
- Never active

These activation states are processed in the following order:

1. Choose a subgroup of connectors that are *active now*.
2. If there is no match, then if any connectors *will become active*, find the subgroup of connectors that will become active soonest (several may become active in five minutes).
3. If there is no match, then if any connectors are *remote initiated*, choose this subgroup of connectors.
4. If there is no match, then use the connectors that are *never active*.

Choosing the Subgroup of Connectors with the Lowest Open Retry Count

Within this subgroup, connectors that are not currently retrying (waiting on an Open Retry timer) are chosen. This approach, known as *preemptive rerouting*, is used so that the MTA does not attempt to route a message to a connector that is known to have not connected the last time it tried.

Suppose that you have a Site Connector and a Dynamic RAS Connector with a higher cost, and the LAN is down. A message is first routed to the Site Connector because it has a lower cost. When the connection fails because the LAN is down, the message is rerouted through the Dynamic RAS Connector. Although the cost is higher, this preemptive rerouting is more likely to achieve timely delivery of the message.

Any new message that comes in before the Open Retry timer has expired on the Site Connector will skip the Site Connector and be routed to the Dynamic RAS Connector first.

1. Within the group that meets the previous criteria, choose a subgroup of connectors with the lowest cost.
2. Within the group that meets the previous criteria, choose a subgroup of local connectors over remote connectors. Site Connectors are counted as local if they are not homed on any particular server; otherwise the Site Connector has an actual locality.

If a connector is remote (as indicated by the Home-MTA attribute), it means that the connector exists on a remote MTA within this site (that is, the message will be routed to that Microsoft Exchange MTA). The MTA selects local connectors first to avoid an extra hop to the remote MTA in the site. Otherwise, no connectors exist to service this address space and the message is marked for NDR for this recipient.

If a non-optimal route (that is, a route that does not have the lowest cost) is chosen because the lowest-cost connectors are down, and the message has not yet been rerouted in the MTA, the MTA performs a *virtual* reroute from the lowest-cost connector to the currently selected connector. This is necessary to prevent loop detection due to circular routes. (When non-optimal routes are chosen, it is possible, and sometimes desirable, for the message to travel circular routes before reaching the final destination.) The example below illustrates why this is necessary.

```
A<-----Cost 1------->B<-----Cost 1----->C<-----Cost 1----->D
A<-----Cost 10----->D
```

A message destined for MTA D will be routed in the following order: A->B->C. However, if the C->D connector is waiting on an Open Retry or is unavailable when the message arrives at C, the MTA on C will route the message to the higher-cost alternate route: C->B->A->D.

Without the virtual reroute at MTA C, the message would be loop-detected when it reentered MTA B. In this situation, it is assumed that the incoming connector will be filtered out of the initial routing attempt for a message (otherwise MTA B would route the message directly back to C due to cost considerations).

Load Balancing

After the final group of connectors has been chosen, the MTA load balances between them. Load balancing is accomplished by randomly choosing one of the connectors in the final group (as they all have equal cost) rather than calculating current queue size, message size, and so on.

After a connector has been routed for a message recipient, it is preferentially routed again when that connector is found in a subsequent recipient's final connector group. This prevents a message for multiple recipients from being routed to the same connector group (because one message has been split into several messages). The first connector chosen from a group is used for later recipients.

If a Site Connector is selected, the Microsoft Exchange MTA load balances between target MTAs through *cost-weighted randomization*. However, cost 0 target MTAs are always tried first, while cost 100 target MTAs are always tried last. Cost-weighted randomization occurs only if routing to all the cost 0 target MTAs has been attempted. All administrator-designated target MTAs are tried on that Site Connector before the message is rerouted to a different connector.

Fan-out

When all recipients have been routed either locally or to a remote connector, the original message is *fanned out* (that is, multiple copies are created, one for each distinct message destination). Each message has the responsibility attribute set for all recipients who have been routed to that destination.

When only a few recipients for a given destination allow for message database encoding format (MDBEF) messages, the message copy for a particular destination is split into two copies. However, this situation is not typical, because conversion on the sending MTA is usually decided based on the properties of the message and the destination MTA/connector, rather than on the per recipient properties.

Conversion Decision

When the MDBEF content type is used, only one address can be included for a message originator/recipient. Although the address can be the DN address or the O/R address, it is usually the DN address. For this reason, DN access for the originator and all recipients is required during conversion. That way, the O/R addresses required by P2 can be obtained. The decision to convert from MDBEF to P2 can only be delayed until the final replicated Microsoft Exchange site (where the MTA can always obtain access to the objects) is referenced by DNs in the message. The decision to convert must be made as soon as possible, to ensure that all information required for the conversion is available.

The main conversion decision process is based on the content type of a message and the destination (either the local MTA or the recipient or remote MTA/connector). As such, it is per-message. However, even if a message is of the MDBEF content type and the chosen connector allows for this content type, an individual *recipient* may not allow MDBEF.

Per-recipient checking is completed during routing to verify whether a particular recipient can support MDBEF. If a recipient is a Microsoft Exchange recipient, it is assumed to support MDBEF. A recipient is assumed to be a Microsoft Exchange recipient if it supports MDBEF and if:

- The remote MTA is a Microsoft Exchange MTA (Site Connector/Dynamic RAS Connector).

- A DN for the recipient is known.

- The recipient is a custom recipient or one-off, and the proxy address matches the connector's Connected Sites routing proxy.

If a recipient is not known to support MDBEF, the message is converted by the conversion decision routine during fan-out. However, the following exceptions override the per-recipient MDBEF determined during routing:

- Inbound conversion always assumes that all recipients support MDBEF.

- XAPI gateways always allow MDBEF.

Result Processing

The result thread receives results for a message indicating:

- Delivery succeed/fail

- Transfer-out succeed/fail

- DL expansion okay

- Routing attempt failed

If transfer-out failed, the message is rerouted. If delivery failed, an attempt is made to reassign the message (that is, *alternate recipient handling* will occur).

If the message is not rerouted or reassigned, checks are made to determine whether a report is required for the recipients. The report is sent only after all responsible recipients have been delivered or transferred successfully, or the MTA is unable to deliver a subset of recipients for some reason. The one exception is that a report is sent immediately for any completely invalid recipients that cannot be routed.

Rerouting and Retries

If a message fails to be sent through its chosen connector, the MTA attempts to reroute the message.

However, there are exceptions:

- If the message is sent to a gateway, no rerouting occurs and the message is considered by the MTA to have been processed to completion.

- If a message is routed to a *never active* or *remote initiated* connector, no rerouting occurs because association is started (unless the activation schedule is changed later).

During rerouting, only the O/R address of the first responsible recipient is used to reroute the message. This is not an optimal solution, because some message recipients may end up traveling a longer path than if they were rerouted individually. However, this reduces the code complexity and processing time required. There are no loop-detect issues, because the rerouting action resets the X.400 loop-detect algorithms.

Every connector has a *retry count* and a *retry interval* that determine how many times, and at what intervals the MTA will try to send a message through each of the connectors. The Site Connector and the Dynamic RAS Connector default to a 10-minute retry interval and a maximum count of 144 retries. On each fan-out message, a copy of the message is stored as a retry count for each connector and target MTA that has been tried.

When a message is routed to a connector that is inaccessible, the retry count for that connector is incremented on the message, and the message is immediately rerouted using the routing and selection process outlined earlier. After all connectors have been tried and the maximum retry count has been encountered, the message will NDR.

For each connector that is tried, if the openconnection fails it will (independently of the message) start an open retry timer to retry the open.

After a message is successfully rerouted, the external and internal trace information for the message is updated to indicate that a reroute has been performed.

Recipient Reassignment

Microsoft Exchange Server does not expose some X.400 alternate-recipient functions, although the Microsoft Exchange MTA supports all these functions. These functions are:

- Recipient-assigned alternate recipient. (Recipient redirects the message to someone else.) This function, which can be disabled by setting the "Recipient_Reassignment_Prohibited" flag in the message, is supported in Microsoft Exchange Server.

- Management domain (MD)-defined alternate recipient (or dead-letter recipient). This can be disallowed by setting the "Alternate_Recipient_Allowed" flag appropriately in the message. This is not supported in the Microsoft Exchange Server Administrator program.

- Originator-requested alternate recipient. The originator requests an alternate recipient to be used if the message would otherwise NDR. This feature is not displayed in the Microsoft Exchange Client information store.

The redirect-and-deliver function is specific to Microsoft Exchange. If this flag is set, a copy of the message is delivered to the recipient *and* to the specified alternate recipient. To maintain X.400 conformance, a delivery receipt is sent only for the copy delivered to the alternate recipient.

Report Handling

Reports are internally generated in three areas:

- Routing
- Result processing
- Recovery

Reports can also be received from remote systems. The routing process for reports is the same as for messages and probes, regardless of the report's origin, except when the report is destined for a DL.

When the report destination is a DL, the MTA backtracks through Originator_ and DL_Expansion_History to find the originator of the message. Each O/R name found by this recursive process in turn becomes the next report destination and is then passed back through the routing process. If the previous entry in this list was a distribution list, the process is repeated until the actual originator is found.

Loop Detection

Loop detection in Microsoft Exchange uses standard X.400 internal and external trace information. It also uses Microsoft Exchange-specific information contained in the per-domain bilateral information of a message or the additional information of a report. This information is used so that multinational enterprises can be supported without undue configuration complexity. In this way, X.400 loop detection triggering can be avoided.

External trace information documents the actions taken on a message, probe, or report by each MD that the message passes through. Each MD the message enters indicates whether the message was relayed or rerouted, plus any Other_Actions (such as redirection or DL expansion) performed by that MD. If the message enters the same MD twice without a reroute, redirection, or DL expansion, the message will be loop detected and will NDR.

Internal trace information is maintained for messages that are routed *within* an MD. Each MTA the message enters indicates whether the message was relayed or rerouted, plus any Other_Actions (such as redirection or DL expansion) performed by that MTA. If the message enters the same MTA twice without a reroute, redirection, or DL expansion, the message will be loop-detected and will NDR. Note that the internal trace information is removed from a message when it is transferred out of an MD.

An X.400 MD is uniquely defined by the c, a, and p components of the O/R address space. These fields are collectively termed the MD's *global domain identifier* (GDI). Because Microsoft Exchange uniquely identifies sites by using the c, a, p, and o components of the O/R address space, it is possible for a message to traverse a site that has the same c, a, and p values as a different site traversed earlier. This would provoke loop detection on the message in a normal X.400 system. To prevent this, each Microsoft Exchange site adds Microsoft Exchange-specific per-domain bilateral information to messages and additional information to reports. This information contains a site DN for the site being traversed.

If a loop is detected in the external trace information, the current site DN is searched for in the Microsoft Exchange-specific information. If the current site DN is not found, it is not a real loop, and therefore X.400 loop detection is suppressed.

Moving Microsoft Exchange Server to Another Computer

It may be necessary to move Microsoft Exchange Server from one computer to a new, more powerful system. This section outlines the steps required to move Microsoft Exchange Server from one computer to another.

You can move a Microsoft Exchange Server from one computer (Server A) to another computer (Server B), assuming:

- The two computer names are unique.
- You have Microsoft Exchange Server, Enterprise Edition or Microsoft Exchange Server, Standard Edition with the Microsoft Exchange Connector.
- Server B is in the same Windows NT domain as Server A, or in a Windows NT domain that has full trust with the domain that contains Server A.

Saving Data on the Original Server (Server A)

It is important to stop all services on Server A and back up the entire Exchsrvr directory. If the logs and database files are on different drives, make sure to back these up as well, or run the Performance Optimizer and move all logs and databases to the Exchsrvr directory where Microsoft Exchange Server was installed.

If you have the Key Management server installed, make sure to back up the Security directory that was created by KM server. This directory is created by default on drive C. Note, however, that the Security directory may not be under the Exchsrvr directory. You also need to back up the KM server startup disk.

The following steps are required to back up your data on the original server.

▶ **To back up data on your server**

1. From the Support\Sample\Csvs\Mailbox directory on the Microsoft Exchange Server compact disc, copy Mailbox.csv to the hard drive.
2. Change the Read-Only attribute on this file.
3. From the Support\Samples\csvs\Dl directory on the Microsoft Exchange Server compact disc, copy Dl.csv to the hard drive.
4. Change the Read-Only attribute on this file.
5. In the Microsoft Exchange Server Administrator window, choose **Directory Export** from the **Tools** menu.
6. In the **Directory Export** dialog box, under **Export objects**, select only the **Mailboxes** check box.
7. Under the **Home Server** list, select Server A.

8. Select the **Include subcontainers** check box, and then select Mailbox.csv as the output file.

9. After export, edit Mailbox.csv and change all occurrences of Server A to Server B. Save the file as Mailbox-Server B.csv.

10. Return to the Microsoft Exchange Administrator window, and from the **Tools** menu, select **Directory Export**.

11. Select only the **Distribution list** check box.

12. Under the **Home Server** list, select **All**.

13. Select the **Include subcontainers** check box, and then select Dl.csv as the output file.

Installing Microsoft Exchange on the New Server (Server B)

Make sure that Server B is in the same Windows NT domain as Server A , or in a domain that has full trust with the domain containing Server A.

Note If you are running Microsoft Exchange Server, Standard Edition without the Microsoft Exchange Connector, follow the steps in the section on moving Microsoft Exchange Server, Standard Edition (later in this chapter), instead of the steps in this section.

---

1. If Server A is a primary domain controller (PDC) and you do not plan to leave it running after moving Microsoft Exchange Server, install Windows NT on Server B and make Server B a backup domain controller (BDC) in the same Windows NT domain as Server A.

2. Install Microsoft Exchange on Server B, joining the Microsoft Exchange site of Server A. Install all the connectors that were installed on Server A.

3. If you are running Microsoft Exchange Server, Standard Edition on Server A, you must install the Microsoft Exchange Connector on Server A before attempting to add Server B to the existing site.

4. Upgrade Server B to the same Microsoft Exchange Service Pack as Server A.

5. All users on Server A should appear in the global address list (GAL) for Server B.

6. In the Administrator window, double-click Server B, and then select the Public Information Store.

7. Choose **Properties** from the **File** menu, and then select the **Instances** tab (this tab is not included in Microsoft Exchange Server, Standard Edition). All of the public folders on Server A should appear.

8. Under the **Public folders** list, select all folders, and then choose **Add** to add all the public folders to the local information store on Server B.

9. By default, the first server in a site will contain and be responsible for the site folders. Site folders consist of the offline Address Book folder, the Microsoft Schedule+ Free/Busy Information folder, and the Organizational Forms folder, if one exists. Other servers installed in the site rely, by default, on the first server for this information. Therefore, if Server A was the first server to be installed in the site, make sure that you have added instances of the Organization Forms, Schedule+ Free/Busy Information, and offline Address Bookfolders to the public information store on Server B.

10. This step ensures that all folders in the site are replicated to Server B. After all steps for moving Server A to Server B are completed, individual public folders can be removed from the public information store on Server B if there are other replicas of these folders on other servers in the same Microsoft Exchange Server site.

11. In the Administrator window, choose a server, and then choose a site.

12. Select **Public Information Store**, then select **Public Folder Resources**.

13. Change the **Public Folder Server** setting to Server B.

14. In the Administrator window, choose **Configuration**.

15. Double-click **DS Site Configuration**.

16. Select the **Offline Address Book** tab.

17. Under the **Offline Address Book server** list, select Server B.

18. In the Administrator window, choose **Configuration**.

19. Double-click **Site Addressing**.

20. Select the **General** tab.

21. Under the **Routing calculation server** list, select Server B.

22. Note that the **Apply** button is not enabled when you select Server B from the **Routing calculation server** list. To enable this button and ensure that the change to the routing calculation server setting is recorded, in the **Display Name** box, add and then remove a character.

23. For each DL defined, select the Distribution List tab and verify that the expansion server is not set to Server A.

Moving Mailboxes to the New Server

This section describes how to move all the mailboxes on Server A to Server B.

Note You can move mailboxes to another server in a site by choosing **Move Mailbox** from the **Tools** menu in the Microsoft Exchange Server Administrator program. However, this only enables you to move the mailboxes to the Recipients container. If this is acceptable, then using the **Move Mailbox** command is the easiest way to move mailboxes.

▶ **To keep the mailboxes in the same containers or subcontainers as they were on Server A**

1. Stop the Information Store service on Server B. In Control Panel, double-click the **Services** icon. Under the **Service** list, select **Microsoft Exchange Information Store,** and then choose **Stop**.

2. In the Exchsrvr\Mdbdata directory on Server B, create a subdirectory called Bak.

3. Move all files from the Exchsrvr\Mbddata directory in Server B to the Bak directory.

4. Copy the Pub.edb file from the Bak directory to the Mbddata directory.

   Before proceeding to the next step, make sure that you completed a backup of the Exchsrvr directory on Server A. This backup should be completed after all services are stopped. Also, verify that you have successfully created the Mailbox-ServerB.csv file.

5. Start all of the Microsoft Exchange services on Server A.

Deleting Mailboxes from the Original Server

Follow the procedure below to delete mailboxes from Server A.

▶ **To delete mailboxes**

1. In the Administrator window for Server A, choose **Server Recipients**.

2. From the menu bar, choose **View**, and then choose **Mailboxes**.

3. Choose Columns, and then add Home Server to the Show the following columns list.

4. Move the position of the Home Server entry so that it is the second entry in the list.

5. Select each container that includes Microsoft Exchange mailboxes.

6. Delete all users who have Server A as their home server.

Recreating Mailboxes on the New Server

Before recreating mailboxes on Server B, make sure that the Microsoft Exchange Directory service is running on Server B.

▶ **To re-create mailboxes**

1. In the Administrator window for Server B, select Server B.

2. In the right pane, double-click **Directory Service**.

3. Choose **Update Now**.

4. Select **Refresh all items in the directory**, and then choose **OK**.

This causes all changes made to the directory on Server A to be replicated to Server B. Note that after the replication is completed, the mailboxes that were deleted from Server A should not be displayed on Server B.

5. In the Administrator window, choose **Directory Import** from the **Tools** menu.

6. Choose **Import File**, and then select the Mailbox-ServerB.csv file.

7. Make sure that the server displayed in the **MS Exchange Server** box is Server B.

8. Under **Account creation**, select **Use select container** if it is not specified in the file. Do not select the **Create Windows NT account** check box.

9. Choose **Import**.

Repeat this step for each file that contains mailbox information. All mailboxes that were originally on Server A should now be re-created on Server B.

Restoring All User Messages on the New Server

Before following the procedure outlined below, make sure that the Microsoft Exchange Directory service is running and that the Microsoft Exchange Information Store service is not running on Server B.

▶ **To restore user messages on the new server**

1. Copy the Priv.edb file from the Mdbdata directory of the Server A backup to the Mdbdata directory on Server B.

Now you should have two files in the Mdbdata directory of Server B: the Privd.edb file that was copied from the Server A backup and the Pub.edb file that was in the Mdbdata directory on Server B.

Do not copy Pub.edb from the Server A backup. There should be no .log or .chk files in the Mdbdata directory of Server B.

2. At the command prompt, switch to the Exchsrver\Bin directory.

3. Type **ISINTEG -Patch**.

4. In Control Panel, double-click the **Services** icon, and then start the Microsoft Exchange Information Store service on Server B.

5. In the Administrator window, select Server B.

6. From the **File** menu, choose **Properties**.

7. Select the **Advanced** tab, select the **All Inconsistencies** option, and then choose **Adjust**.

All mailboxes should now be migrated to Server B. As long as the Microsoft Exchange Directory service is running on Server A, all users should be able to log on to the Microsoft Exchange Client by using their old profiles. Even though the profiles point to Server A, the Microsoft Exchange Directory service on Server A automatically redirects the client to Server B and the profile is modified to point to Server B.

Recreating DLs on the New Server

You only need to re-create DLs if you have manually moved the mailboxes to Server B. This is because the process of manually moving the mailboxes involved deleting the users on Server A. When you did this, the users were removed from the DLs. This is also the reason why all the DLs were exported.

▶ **To re-create the DLs**

1. In the Administrator window, choose **Directory Import** from the **Tools** menu.

2. Select the Dl.csv files, and then choose **Import**.

Moving the KM Server

The following steps are applicable only if you already have the KM server running on Server A and security is enabled for the Microsoft Exchange mailboxes on Server A.

▶ **To move the KM server**

1. Remove the KM server from Server A.

2. In Control Panel, double-click **Services**, and then stop the Key Management Server service on Server A.

3. In the Exchkm directory on the Microsoft Exchange Server compact disc, run Setup.exe.

4. Install the KM server on Server B. Select the option to create a startup disk.

5. After the installation is completed, stop the Key Management Server service on Server B.

6. From the KM Server Startup disk for Server A, copy the Kmspwd.ini file onto another disk for Server B. Label this disk "KM Server Startup Disk: Server B."

7. From the backup of the Security directory on Server A, copy the Security\Mgrent directory to the Security directory of Server B.

8. Insert the new KM Server Startup disk for Server B (labeled "KM Server Startup Disk: Server B") into the disk drive on Server B.

9. On Server B, start the Key Management Server service.

10. As long as the .epf files are still on your users' computers and their profiles have not changed, your users can read all previously encrypted mail.

Moving the Microsoft Mail Connector

The following steps are applicable if you have the Microsoft Mail Connector installed on Server A.

▶ **To move the Microsoft Mail Connector**

1. Run the Microsoft Exchange Administrator program for Server A, noting the settings for the Microsoft Mail Connector.

2. On Server A, stop the Microsoft Mail Connector Interchange, any Microsoft Mail PCMTA services, and the Directory Synchronization service.

3. Make sure that the Microsoft Mail Connector is installed on Server B. If it isn't, install it.

4. On Server B, configure the Microsoft Mail Connector exactly as it was configured on Server A.

Moving the Directory Synchronization Configuration

The following procedure describes how to move the directory synchronization configuration to the new server.

▶ **To move the directory synchronization configuration**

1. In the Administrator window for Server B, choose **Directory Replication**, then double-click on the connector to display the properties for the Directory Synchronization Server object.

2. Change the Server setting to Server B. When you do so, the following warning message appears:

   "Changing the server in Responsible DXA can cause the loss of Directory Synchronization information. A full export of Directory Synchronization information will occur in the next scheduled cycle."

3. Choose **OK** to dismiss the warning, and then choose **OK** again to close the tab.

4. Run the Microsoft Mail Administrator program for each Microsoft Mail requester postoffice. Select **Config**, **DirSync**, **Requestor**, **Export**, then **Import**.

5. On Server B, start the Microsoft Mail Connector Interchange service, any Microsoft Mail PCMTA services, and the Directory Synchronization service.

At the next scheduled time, Microsoft Mail and Microsoft Exchange will be resynchronized.

Moving the Directory Synchronization Requester

1. In the Administrator window for Server B, right-click the Directory Synchronization Requester object to display its properties.

2. Change the Server setting to Server B. When you do so, the following warning message appears:

   "Changing the server in Responsible DXA can cause the loss of Directory Synchronization information. A full export of Directory Synchronization information will occur on the new Responsible DXA in the next scheduled cycle."

3. Choose **OK** to dismiss the warning, and then choose **OK** again.

4. Select the **Requester** tab, select **Full Export,** and then select **Import on the Next Cycle**.

Moving X.400 Connectors

Follow the steps below if you have one or more X.400 Connectors installed on Server A.

▶ **To move X.400 Connectors**

1. On Server B, install the required MTA transport stacks.

2. On Server B, display the properties for each X.400 Connector.

3. Change the MTA transport stack so that it is a stack installed on Server B.

4. On Server A, delete the MTA transport stacks.

5. On Server B, request a full directory update.

6. On the directory service object under **Configuration**, **Servers**, **Server B**, choose **Update Now**, and then select **Refresh all items in the directory**.

Moving Directory Replication Connectors

Follow the steps below if you want to move directory replication connects.

▶ **To move directory replication connectors**

1. On Server B, display the properties of each directory replication connector.

2. Change the local bridgehead server to Server B, if it is currently Server A. Note that you may need to change the remote bridgehead settings on the remote directory replication connector, if the remote server is not available on the network.

Moving the Internet Mail Service

Reconfigure each Internet Mail Service on Server B.

Moving Third-Party Connectors

Reinstall all third-party connectors installed on Server A.

Microsoft Exchange Client Profiles

Make sure that both Server A and Server B are running. Server A should be kept running until every client has logged on at least once. This ensures that the Microsoft Exchange Client profiles are automatically redirected to Server B instead of Server A, thus eliminating the need to manually modify client profiles.

After all clients have logged on to Microsoft Exchange Server at least once, use the steps below to remove Server A from the organization. If Server A is removed before all clients have logged on, the profile on the clients will need to be modified to point to Server B.

Removing the Original Server from the Organization

Use the procedure below to remove Server A from the organization.

▶ **To remove Server A**

1. In the Administrator window for Server A, select **Public Information Store**.
2. From the **File** menu, choose **Properties**.
3. Select the **Instances** tab.
4. Remove all public folder instances from this store.
5. On Server A, run the Microsoft Exchange Server Setup program, and then remove the installed connectors.
6. Run the Microsoft Exchange Administrator program in raw mode.
7. From the **View** menu, choose **All**.
8. Select the Recipients container. In the right pane, select **Microsoft Schedule+ Free/Busy Connector**.
9. From the **File** menu, choose **Raw Properties**.
10. Change every occurrence from Server A to Server B to include the computer name, display name, home MDB, and home MTA. Note that you must choose **Set** to ensure that these changes will take effect.

11. In the Administrator window for Server B, select Server A, and then press the DELETE key. When you do so, a warning message appears stating that there is still one mailbox and gateway on Server A. This warning refers to the system attendant mailbox on Server A, which can be safely deleted.

12. Choose **Yes**. When you do so, another warning appears:

    "The contents of all public folder instances on this server will be deleted. Are you sure you want to delete server 'Server A'?"

14. Choose **Yes**.

Server A will be deleted from the Microsoft Exchange Directory on Server B, and all data has been moved from Server A to Server B.

Moving Microsoft Exchange Server, Standard Edition

With Microsoft Exchange Server, Standard Edition, it is not possible to have more than one server in a site or to connect Microsoft Exchange Server sites. To move Microsoft Exchange Server from one server computer (Server A) to another (Server B), follow the procedures described in this section.

1. Install the Microsoft Exchange Connector on Server A. Note that this software must be purchased separately.

2. Follow the steps outlined earlier in this chapter.

If it is not possible to use the Microsoft Exchange Connector, follow the steps below to move Microsoft Exchange Server from Server A to Server B. After the move from Server A to Server B, all Microsoft Exchange Clients will need their profiles modified to point from Server B to Server A.

Backing Up Data

Before moving Server A to Server B, follow the steps below to back up your data on Server A.

▶ **To back up Microsoft Exchange Server data**

1. Stop all Microsoft Exchange Server services on Server A and back up the entire Exchsrv subdirectory. If the logs and database files are on different drives, back up these directories as well.

2. If the KM server is installed, back up the Security directory.

3. From the KM Server Startup disk, back up the Kmpswd.ini file.

4. Start all Microsoft Exchange services on Server A.

Exporting Mailboxes, Custom Recipients, and DLs

To export mailboxes, custom recipients and distribution lists, follow the steps below.

1. From the Support\Samples\Csvs\Mailbox directory on the Microsoft Exchange Server compact disc, copy the Mailbox.csv file to your computer.

2. From the Support\Samples\Csvs\Custom directory on the same compact disc, copy the Custom.csv file to your computer.

3. From the Support\Samples\Csvs\Dl directory on the same compact disc, copy the Dl.csv file to your computer.

4. For each of these three files:

   In Windows NT Explorer, from the **File** menu, choose **Properties**, and then clear the **Read-Only** check box.

▶ **To export the Mailbox.csv file**

1. In the Administrator window for Server A, choose **Directory Export** from the **Tools** menu.

2. Choose **Export File**, and then select Mailbox.csv.

3. Choose **Container**, and then select the Recipients container.

4. Under **Export objects**, select the **Mailbox** check box.

5. Choose **Export**.

6. Edit the Mailbox.csv file, replacing all instances of Server A with Server B.

7. Save the file.

Repeat these steps for each top-level container. Use different file names for each top-level container and do not specify Mailbox.csv as a file.

▶ **To export the Custom.csv file**

1. In the Administrator window, choose **Directory Export** from the **Tools** menu.

2. Choose **Export File**, and then select Custom.csv.

3. Choose **Container**, and then select the **Global Address List** container.

4. Under **Export objects**, select the **Custom Recipient** check box.

5. Choose **Export**.

▶ **To export the Dl.csv file**

1. In the Administrator window, choose **Directory Export** from the **Tools** menu.

2. Choose **Export File**, and then select Dl.csv.

3. Choose **Container**, and then select the **Global Address List** container.

4. Under **Export objects**, select the **Distribution list** check box.

5. Choose **Export**.

Saving Directory Synchronization Configuration Information

If you are using the Microsoft Mail Connector and have directory synchronization set up with Microsoft Mail postoffices, follow the steps below to save directory synchronization configuration information.

▶ **To save directory synchronization information**

- If Microsoft Exchange is the dirsync server, note the names of the dirsync server and each remote requester. Also note the Import and Export containers for each remote requester.

- If Microsoft Exchange is a dirsync requester, then note the exact name of the requester and the **Import/Export** containers.

This information must be available when recreating the directory synchronization objects on the new server. You need to re-create the dirsync server and requester exactly as they were defined on Server A to preserve DLs containing Microsoft Mail custom recipients that were previously dirsync'd into Microsoft Exchange Server. The custom recipients need to be re-created in the same container, with the same directory name and DN. This is only possible by importing the exported custom recipient data from the old server. By importing the custom recipient and DL information, you will retrieve all the old custom recipients and DLs.

However, if the dirsync requesters (or remote requesters) were not created with identical names, the Microsoft Mail custom recipients will not be associated with the new requesters. These custom recipients will never be deleted automatically as part of directory synchronization, even if the user has been deleted from the Microsoft Mail postoffice. To maintain the old directory synchronization information, the dirsync requester's server must have the same names, and must create new custom recipients in the same container.

You cannot just copy over the Exchsrvr directory from Server A to Server B, because the Microsoft Exchange directory file (Dir.edb) contains the name of the server. Because the computer names of the source (Server A) and target (Server B) computers are different, you cannot use the Dir.edb file from Server A on Server B. Due to this restriction, all information in the Microsoft Exchange directory must be re-created on Server B.

Saving Public Folders

Follow the procedure below to save your public folders.

▶ **To save public folders**

1. Log on to the Microsoft Exchange Client by using an account on Server A that has at least Read access to all public folders. If necessary, use the Administrator program to grant this access permission on public folders.

2. Add "Personal Folders" to the current profile using PublicFoldersOnServerA.pst as the file name.

3. Create a new personal folder called "Public Folders on Server A."

4. Select all public folders and copy them to the Public Folders on Server A folder that you just created. This should also copy any forms associated with the public folders.

Saving Organizational Forms

If you have organization-wide forms, follow the procedure below.

▶ **To save your organizational forms**

1. While still in the Microsoft Exchange Client, create a new personal folder called "OrgForms."

2. Select the new folder.

3. From the **File** menu, choose **Properties**.

4. Select the **Forms** tab.

5. Choose **Set**, and then select **Organization Forms**. This is the name of the folder that was specified using the Microsoft Exchange Administrator program (under **Tools\Forms Administrator**).

6. Select all the forms listed in the list on the left, and with all the forms highlighted, choose **Copy**. This copies all the selected forms to the list on the right. All the forms in the list are then copied to the OrgForms personal folder that you created in step one.

7. Repeat these steps for each forms library.

As mentioned earlier, you cannot copy the Pub.edb file from Server A to Server B and expect all the public folders to be available on Server B. After you copy Pub.edb to Server B, and run the ISINTEG troubleshooting utility and the DS/IS consistency adjuster, the public folders on Server A will still not be available on Server B. Only after you display the public information store properties on Server B, select the **Instances** tab and add all the public folders to be homed on Server B, will these folders be available.

Note   The **Instances** tab is not available with Microsoft Exchange Server, Standard Edition. Because Standard Edition servers are stand-alone servers, they do not have the ability to store replicas of public folders.

Installing Microsoft Exchange Server

On Server B, install Microsoft Exchange Server with the same organization and site names as the Microsoft Exchange installation on Server A. Also, you must install any Service Packs that were installed on Server A.

Installing the KM Server

Follow the procedure below to install the KM server:

▶ **To install the KM server**

1. If you were using the KM server on Server A, install the KM server on Server B. Select the option to create a startup disk. After the installation is completed, stop the Key Management service on Server B.

2. From the KM Server Startup disk for Server A, copy the Kmspwd.ini file to another disk for Server B. Label this disk "KM Server Startup Disk: Server B."

3. On the new server, rename the Security\Mgrent subdirectory to Mgrent.original.

4. From the backup of the Security directory on Server A, copy the Security\Mgrent directory to the Security directory of Server B.

5. Insert the new KM Server Startup disk for Server B (labeled "KM Server Startup Disk: Server B") into the disk drive on Server B.

6. Start the Key Management Server service on Server B.

Re-creating Mailboxes, Custom Recipients, and DLs

Follow the procedure below to re-create your mailbox, custom recipients, and distribution list files.

▶ **To re-create mailboxes, custom recipients, and DLs**

1. Start the Microsoft Exchange Administrator program for Server B.

2. Recreate the same containers as you did for Server A.

3. From the **Tools** menu, choose **Directory Import**.

4. Import the Mailbox.csv file, and any other files that were previously created.

5. Import the Custom.csv file.

6. Import the file DL.csv file.

All the mailboxes, custom recipients, and DLs from Server A should now be re-created on Server B.

Restoring User Messages

Follow the procedure below to restore user messages:

▶ **To restore user messages**

1. On Server B, make sure that the Microsoft Exchange Directory service is running and that the Microsoft Exchange Information Store service is not running.

2. On Server B, rename the Mdbdata subdirectory under the Exchsrvr directory to Mdbdata.original.

3. On Server B, create a new directory called Mdbdata under the Exchsrvr directory.

4. Copy the Pub.edb file from the Mdbdata.original directory to the Mdbdata directory.

   At this stage, the Mdbdata directory should contain only the Pub.edb file.

5. From the Mdbdata directory of the backup of Server A, copy the Priv.edb file to the Mdbdata directory of Server B.

   Now you should have two files in the Mdbdata directory of Server B: the Priv.edb file that was copied from the Server A backup and the Pub.edb file that was in the Mdbdata directory of Server B.

Note   Do not copy the Pub.edb file from the Server A backup.

There should be no .log or .chk files in the Mdbdata directory of Server B.

1. At the command prompt, switch to the Exchsrvr\bin directory, and type the following command to run the ISINTEG troubleshooting utility:

   ISINTEG -patch

2. On Server B, start the Microsoft Exchange Information Store service.

3. In the Administrator window for Server B, select Server B.

4. From the **File** menu, choose **Properties**.

5. Select the **Advanced** tab.

6. Select **All inconsistencies**, and then choose **Adjust**.

Restoring Organizational Forms

Follow the procedure below to restore your organizational forms.

▶ **To restore your organizational forms**

1. In the Administrator window of Server B, choose **Forms Administrator** from the **Tools** menu.

2. Choose **New**. If your Forms Library is called "Organization Forms," accept the default value in the **Library folder name** box; otherwise, type the correct library name.

3. After you have selected the correct library name, choose **OK**, and then choose **Close** to close the **Organization Forms Library Administrator** dialog box.

4. If you have more than one forms library, repeat steps two and three to re-create each library.

5. In the left pane of the Administrator window, select **Folders**, **System Folders**, **EFORMS REGISTRY**.

6. In the right pane, select the forms library that you created in steps two and three. The default name should be "Organization Forms."

7. From the **File** menu, choose **Properties**.

8. Select the **General** tab, and then choose **Client Permissions**.

9. Add your Microsoft Exchange mailbox with the Owner role.

10. Close all open dialog boxes.

11. Repeat steps for each forms library that you created.

12. Quit the Administrator program.

13. Log on to the Microsoft Exchange Client against Server B.

14. Add the Personal Folders Information service to the client profile. Select the PublicFoldersOnServerA.pst file that you created earlier. This .pst file should contain two folders: "Public Folders on Server A" and "OrgForms," the forms library that you created.

15. In the Microsoft Exchange Client Viewer, select the OrgForms folder.

16. From the **File** menu, choose **Properties**.

17. Select the **Forms** tab, and then choose **Manage**.

18. Choose **Set**, and then select all the forms displayed in the list on the right.

19. Choose **Copy**.

All the forms should now be copied from the .pst file to the server-based Organization Forms folder and should be available to users.

Restoring Public Folders

Use the following procedure to restore your public folders

▶ **To restore public folders**

1. Make sure that you are logged on to the Microsoft Exchange Client.

2. Select the Public Folders on Server A folder.

3. The folder contents list (right pane of Microsoft Exchange Server) should contain all the subfolders under the Public Folders on Server A folder. Select all of these subfolders and copy them to the All Public Folders folder.

Reconfiguring Directory Synchronization

If you are using the Microsoft Mail Connector to communicate with Microsoft Mail postoffices, you need to reconfigure the Microsoft Mail Connector on Server B exactly as it was on Server A.

Microsoft Exchange as the Directory Synchronization Server

If Microsoft Exchange was the dirsync server on Server A, reconfigure Server B to be the dirsync server. Use the same settings as on Server A, including the name. Reconfigure all remote dirsync requesters exactly as they were on Server A. Make sure that the requester names and Import/Export containers are all the same.

1. Start the Microsoft Mail Administrator program for each Microsoft Mail requester postoffice, and then select **Configuration**, **Dirsync**, **Requestor**, **Export** and **Import**.

2. On Server B, start the Microsoft Mail Connector Interchange service, any Microsoft Mail PCMTA services, and the Directory Synchronization service.

At the next scheduled time, the Microsoft Mail and Microsoft Exchange Server should be resynchronized again.

Reconfiguring Microsoft Exchange Server as a Dirsync Requester

If Microsoft Exchange was a dirsync requester on Server A, reconfigure Server B to be a dirsync requester with the same settings as Server A.

▶ **To reconfigure Microsoft Exchange Server as a dirsync requester**

1. Select the **Requester** tab.

2. Choose **Settings**, and then select **Full Export** and **Full Import**.

Regenerating the Offline Address Book

The offline Address Book will not be migrated automatically to Server B. It must be reconfigured and regenerated on Server B.

▶ **To regenerate the offline Address Book on Server B**

1. Verify that Microsoft Exchange Server is running.
2. In the Administrator window, choose **Configuration**.
3. Double-click **DS Site Configuration**.
4. Select the **Offline Address Book** tab.
5. Select the correct container, and then choose **Generate Offline Address Book Now**.

Schedule+ Free/Busy Data

The Schedule+ Free/Busy information cannot be migrated to Server B. However, this information is regenerated automatically when users make changes to their calendars.

Moving the Internet Mail Service

Reconfigure each Internet Mail Service on Server B.

Moving Third-Party Connectors

All third-party connectors installed on Server A must be reinstalled on Server B.

Microsoft Exchange Client Profiles

All Microsoft Exchange Client profiles must be modified to point to Server A rather than Server B.

▶ **To modify the client profile**

1. In Control Panel, double-click the **Mail** icon, and then choose **Show Profiles**.
2. Select the profile to be modified, and then choose **Properties**.

3. Select **Microsoft Exchange Server** from the list of information services, and then choose **Properties**.

4. Change the Microsoft Exchange Server name to Server B.

Note   After a profile is modified, offline folder files (.ost) files are not accessible. Normally, a copy of all information in the .ost file is saved in the user's private mailbox on the server . If mail in the .ost file must be saved, *before* modifying the profile or connecting to the old server, the user must run the Microsoft Exchange Client in offline mode, and then copy all required messages and/or folders to a .pst file. If the user tries to connect to the old server or modifies the profile with the new server name, the .ost file will not be accessible. For security reasons, it is not possible to recover data from an ost file.

Moving Details Templates

Use the procedure below to move details templates.

▶ **To move details templates**

1. On Server A, create a directory called Templates.

2. From the Support\Samples\Tpl directory on the Microsoft Exchange Server compact disc, copy Tpl.ini and Tpl.csv to your Templates directory on Server A.

3. Remove the Read-Only attributes from these files.

4. Edit the Tpl.ini file. Under the [Import] and [Export] sections, modify the Basepoint entry by replacing the words "ORG" and "SITE" with your organization and site names. Save the file.

5. At the command prompt, switch to the Templates directory and type the following:

   C:\Exchsrvr\BIN\ADMIN /e tpl.csv /d Server A /o tpl.ini

6. Copy the Templates directory from Server A to Server B.

7. On Server B, at the command prompt, type the following:

   C:\Exchsrvr\BIN\ADMIN /i tpl.csv /d Server B /o tpl.ini.

If Both Computers Have the Same Name

Follow the procedures below if you are moving Microsoft Exchange Server from one computer to another computer that has the same name.

The steps in this section apply if the new Microsoft Exchange Server computer is in:

- The same Windows NT domain as the Microsoft Exchange Server computer to be moved; or
- A domain that has a two-way trust relationship with the Windows NT domain that contains the Microsoft Exchange Server computer to be moved.

Verifying That a Domain Controller Is Available

Before moving Microsoft Exchange Server to the new computer, verify that the computer to be replaced is not the only Windows NT domain controller in the domain. After this computer is brought down as part of the procedure to move Microsoft Exchange Server, there must another domain controller that can validate Windows NT logon requests.

Moving a Primary Domain Controller Computer

If Microsoft Exchange Server is being moved from a primary domain controller (PDC) computer, make sure there is at least one other backup domain controller (BDC) in the Windows NT domain. After bringing down the computer to be moved, upgrade the BDC to become a PDC.

Moving a BDC Computer

If the computer to be moved is a BDC, make sure that the PDC in the domain is running and operational, or at a minimum, that there are other BDC computers that can be upgraded to become the PDC.

Moving Microsoft Exchange Server to Another Computer with the Same Hardware Platform

The steps below describe how to move Microsoft Exchange Server to a new computer that has the same hardware platform as the original computer. For purposes of this example, the two computers will be referred to as the Original Server and the New Server, even though both computers have the same NetBIOS computer name.

▶ **To back up information from the Original Server**

1. Start the Microsoft Exchange Administrator program on the Original Server. Make note of the organization and site names.

2. On the Original Server, stop all Microsoft Exchange Server services.

3. Copy the entire Exchsrvr directory to another computer on the network, or to a tape drive. If the Microsoft Exchange Server log and database directories are on different drives, use the Performance Optimizer or the Microsoft Exchange Administrator program to move all the directories to their corresponding locations under the Exchsrvr directory where Microsoft Exchange was installed. This should be done before backing up the Exchsrvr directory.

4. If the KM Server is installed, stop the Key Management Server service and back up the Security directory. Back up the KM Server Service Startup disk as well.

5. Shut down the Original Server. As mentioned earlier, make sure that there is an operational domain controller in the Windows NT domain.

Installing Windows NT and Microsoft Exchange Server on the New Server

Use the following procedure to install Windows NT and Microsoft Exchange Server on the New Server. Before you install Windows NT on the New Server, make sure that the Original Server has been turned off.

▶ **To install Windows NT and Microsoft Exchanger Server**

1. Install Windows NT on the New Server with the same computer name as the Original Server. If necessary, make it a BDC.

2. On the New Server, at the command prompt, type **Setup /R** to install Microsoft Exchange Server.

3. Use the same organization and site names that were used on the Original Server. Also, make sure to install all connectors that were installed on the Original Server. To do so, select the **Custom** installation option.

4. During setup, when prompted for the Microsoft Exchange service account, select the same service account that you used for the Original Server. This must be done because if a new service account is selected after the directory from the Original Server is restored over the New Server, the new service account will not have permissions on the directory.

5. Do not run the Performance Optimizer at the end of the Setup program.

6. Make sure that no Microsoft Exchange Server services are running.

Re-creating Data from the Original Microsoft Exchange Server on the New Server

Use the following procedure to re-create data on the New Server.

▶ **To re-create data**

1. From the backed-up Exchsrvr directory on the Original Server, copy all the files over the Exchsrvr directory on the New Server.

Note If the Original Server and the New Server do not have the same hardware platform, do *not* copy the contents of the entire Exchsrver directory over the New Server. If you do so, you will destroy your executable files. For more information on how to re-create data on a new server that does not have the same hardware platform, see the "Moving Microsoft Exchange Server to Another Computer with a Different Hardware Platform" section.

---

2. Start the Microsoft Exchange System Attendant and Microsoft Exchange Directory services.

3. At the Windows NT command prompt, type the following to run the ISINTEG troubleshooting utility:

   ISINTEG -patch

4. Start the Microsoft Exchange Server Information Store service.

5. In the Administrator window, select the New Server.

6. From the **File** menu, choose **Properties**.

7. Select the **Advanced** tab, select **All Inconsistencies**, and then choose **Adjust**.

Installing the KM Server

Follow the procedure below to install the KM server:

▶ **To install the KM server**

1. If you were using the KM server on the Original Server, install the KM server on the New Server.

2. Select the option to create a startup disk. After the installation is completed, stop the Key Management Server service on the New Server.

3. From the KM Server Startup disk for the Original Server, copy the Kmsp.ini file to another disk. Label this disk "KM Server Startup Disk: New Server."

4. On the New Server, rename the \Mgrent subdirectory under the Security directory to Mgrent.original.

5. From the backup of the Security directory on the Original Server, copy the Security\Mgrent directory to the Security directory of the New Server.

6. Insert the new KM Server Startup disk for the New Server (labeled "KM Server Startup Disk: New Server") into the disk drive on the New Server.

7. Start the Key Management Server service on the New Server.

8. Run the Performance Optimizer to make the appropriate changes.

9. Start all the Microsoft Exchange Server services.

Connectors

Restore all Site Connector and X.400 Connector information on the New Server. Any Microsoft Mail, Internet Mail Service, or Dynamic RAS Connectors must be reconfigured. If you use third-party connectors, those also need to be reconfigured.

Microsoft Exchange Client Profiles

Microsoft Exchange Server should now be running on the New Server in the same way it was on the Original Server. Microsoft Exchange clients should be able to connect to the New Server in the same way as they connected to the Original Server.

Moving Microsoft Exchange Server to Another Computer with a Different Hardware Platform

Follow the steps outlined in the "Moving Microsoft Exchange Server to Another Computer with the Same Hardware Platform" section. However, rather than copying the entire Exchsrvr directory from the Original Server to the New Server, do the following.

From your backed-up copy of the Exchsrvr directory of the Original Server, copy the following subdirectories to the Exchsrvr directory on the New Server: Dsadata, Dxadata, Imcdata, Mdbdata, and Mtadata. If you overwrote all the files from the Exchsrvr directory of the Original Server, you would destroy your executable files.

CHAPTER 3

Optimizing Performance

Your system's performance is also affected by the server's software and hardware configurations. You can minimize performance bottlenecks by balancing server hardware resources to support the expected load and adjusting software settings. This chapter suggests ways you can maximize the number of users supported while keeping response times low. Keep in mind that if you are supporting a live user population, you must be more cautious with the changes you make.

For information about troubleshooting performance, see Chapter 7, "Troubleshooting Microsoft Exchange Server." For more information about optimizing performance, see the *Microsoft Exchange Server Concepts and Planning Guide*.

Performance Tuning Microsoft Exchange Server

To performance tune Microsoft Exchange Server, you need to define how your system is used. There are different configuration recommendations depending on the role of your server. For example, does your server support user mailboxes? Or does it serve as a messaging hub or mail gateway?

It is always a good idea to try to understand the workload being placed on the system by asking this question: What are your users doing? To gather user profile information, you can use the StorStat tool, which is available in the Exchange directory on the Microsoft BackOffice Resource Kit, Part Two compact disc. This tool can help greatly by providing you with sizing information.

Ultimately, you must examine the behavior of the system while it is in operation. You can do so by using the Windows NT Performance Monitor (PerfMon) tool. For more information on this tool, see the Windows NT Resource Kit. Performance Monitor enables you to observe important factors that affect the server's behavior, such as *workloads* (How many messages per second are arriving?) and *resource demands* (How much CPU time is being used? How much memory?). The information is presented as performance counters, which you can monitor in real time or collect in .log files for later analysis. When you examine the demand on resources, you can generally see what needs to be done to improve response times or throughputs.

You can use the Microsoft Exchange Server Load Simulator (Loadsim.exe) to conduct system sizing experiments prior to deployment. Load Simulator emulates a large number of client computers and places a very realistic load on the server so that you can see how it behaves and what response times to expect. Although this section does not describe the Load Simulator tool in detail, if you are conducting a Load Simulator experiment, the information provided here will help you.

Run the Performance Optimizer (PerfWiz) after you install Microsoft Exchange Server and any time you make configuration changes on the server. The Performance Optimizer is available on the Microsoft Exchange Server compact disc. The Performance Optimizer optimally adjusts a number of system settings for any hardware in the server.

Server Roles

This section discusses roles a server might fill in your messaging topology. For each role, general recommendations have been made. These recommendations are based on the assumption that you want to deploy a server with the highest possible capacity. If you don't need to "max out" the server, you may not need to follow some of these recommendations.

Servers That Primarily Support Users

The following areas are discussed to help you improve performance on servers that are primarily supporting users.

- The disk subsystem
- CPU subsystem
- Memory and network capacity

The disk subsystem

In the most common customer configurations, the disk subsystem and memory are the first resources to become saturated in a Microsoft Exchange Server computer. One significant thing you can do to improve disk performance is to get the information store log files on to their own physical disks, apart from other files in the system. Because the logs are always sequentially written, having dedicated disks means that the disk heads won't be randomized by other activities. They will always be in the right place for the next write. And because seeking is the slowest thing a disk does, this is a big help.

The information store database files, on the other hand, are randomly accessed. In this case, the best thing you can do is to put the disks in a RAID array for maximum random access performance.

You can improve performance by using good disk controllers. Caching controllers increases your disk's performance for reading, and if the controller has battery backups, this can improve write performance as well. If the controller works as a write cache (or caches writes) then it must be battery backed up. Problems with cache writes (for example, in the event of a power outage) will cause the computer to lose data. Batteries are on the card to keep data on the card backed up. If the data is cached and there is a power outage, the data will be saved, not lost. Make sure that you don't put so many disks on one controller that the controller becomes a bottleneck.

It is important to consider the reliability of these disks, because your users will be depending on them. It may be wise to mirror the log files, and to use RAID 5 on the database.

Recommendations

- Use the fastest possible disks for the information store log and database.
- Use dedicated disks for information store logs.
- Stripe the information store database.
- Use a sufficient number of high-performance controllers.

CPU subsystem

After disks and memory, the next most likely resource to become saturated is the CPU.

Use the fastest possible CPUs. If the server supports only users and does not run connectors and other processes, there are limits to how much work you can offload by adding CPUs. If the server performs other processing functions, there is a definite benefit to adding more processors. For example, it may be useful to add processors if your server supports connectors or doubles as a messaging hub, domain controller, or SQL Server database.

To make the best use of your processors, use a large L2 cache. This keeps the processor from waiting while data is retrieved from main memory. Also, in a multiprocessor server, the cache keeps load off the system bus, which improves your overall throughput.

Recommendations

- Use the fastest available CPUs.
- Use multiprocessor-ready computers.
- Use the largest available caches.

Optimizing memory and network capacity

Two other resources that can be saturated are memory and network capacity. If the system is thrashing (that is, if there is excessive paging), it will be obvious. If it's not thrashing, you will not notice paging at all. Not enough memory in the system will cause the system to thrash. Fortunately, it is easy to add memory to correct this.

If there is not enough *network capacity* (bandwidth) between the users and the server, your efforts to provide a responsive server will be unsuccessful. The network will be your bottleneck.

When local area network (LAN) connectivity is used, you have the option to replace a 10 MB Ethernet with 100 MB.

In a wide area network (WAN) scenario, there are two important things to note. First, this type of traffic is very bursty (characterized by large bursts of activity). It is not unusual to see peak usage several times the average. Second, bandwidth demand varies widely from company to company and site to site. You may see wide range characteristics of per usage bandwith utilization, depending on the usage patterns. It is typical for server-to-client traffic to be three to four times the client-to-server traffic, because the server responses to client requests are bigger than the requests themselves.

Recommendations

- Ensure adequate memory. If your system is paging excessively, it is a good indication that you need more memory in the computer. You can fix thrashing by adding more memory or removing the load on the server.

- Ensure adequate network bandwidth.

Servers That Support Connectors

The following tasks create additional work for a server:

- Connecting sites by using the Site Connector, X.400 Connector or Internet Mail Service.

- Connecting to other types of messaging systems (by using the Internet Mail Service, X.400 Connector, Microsoft Exchange Connector for Lotus cc:Mail, and so on).

- Supporting protocols requiring content conversion such as post office protocol version 3 (POP3), network news transfer protocol (NNTP), or hypertext transfer protocol (HTTP).

The message transfer agent (MTA), for example, will be involved when connectors are used. The MTA secures all messages to disk, so if there is a lot of traffic, disk input and output can become important. One option is to provide a separate disk for MTA files; another is to maintain the MTA files in the stripe set with the information store database. The same is true for the Internet Mail Service because it also secures messages to disk.

Make sure that you have adequate network bandwidth to carry the traffic. Connector traffic will often be carried over WAN links, and as mentioned earlier, the traffic patterns can vary widely from company to company. Use the Network Monitor to verify that you have capacity available on the links.

Most connectors require the system to send and receive messages in a format that is different from the storage format. Mapping content from the storage format into another format or protocol is a CPU-intensive task that may benefit from more processors.

Recommendations

- Use a separate disk for MTA queues, or place them in a stripe set with the information store database.

- Use a separate disk for Internet Mail Service queues, or place them in a stripe set with the information store database.

- Ensure adequate bandwidth between sites.

- Consider adding more processors.

Public Folder Servers

The usage patterns for public folders vary from company to company. Some don't use public folders, others support discussion groups and news in public folders, and others deploy intensive workflow applications. If your organization supports large-scale public folder activity, keep in mind that the *public information store* is a separate database from the *private information stor*e. It has its own database file. This means that you can maintain the public information store database files on a logical drive that is separate from the private information database, for maximum random I/O performance. Likewise, you can maintain the public store database on a separate drive, although this is less likely to increase performance if you already have a stripe set for the database. The 16 GB limit on the private and public stores are separate, so the public store space isn't counted against the 16 GB limit of the private store, and vice versa.

Many site administrators may want to provide Internet newsgroups or Usenet, and store this data in public folders for uniform user access. In such a case, the incoming news may generate a large amount of write activity in the public store, so be sure to optimize the log drives.

Although the public and private stores are separate databases, a single instance of the database engine runs both. They share the same memory buffers. If your organization experiences heavy use of public folders, you can improve performance by splitting the public folders onto separate servers. This reduces contention for computer resources, including buffers. A pool of public folder servers can also provide flexibility in load balancing.

Recommendations

- Understand your usage pattern.
- If there is a large amount of read activity, focus on information store public database disks.
- If there is a large amount of write activity, focus on information store public log disks.
- Consider using a pool of public folder servers.

Servers That Support Other Loads

If your organization supports Microsoft Exchange Server in combination with other applications such as SQL Server, or if you use file and print services or domain controllers, you must benchmark the workload and configuration you expect to run. This is the only reliable way to determine the system performance under the expected load. Load Simulator is available to emulate the Microsoft Exchange Server part of the workload.

Introduction to Bottlenecks

This section discusses the concept of a bottleneck. The term "bottleneck" is used in various ways by many people. The precise definition that will be used here enables you to take appropriate action if a bottleneck is a problem on your server.

What Is a Bottleneck?

The *bottleneck* in a system is the service center with the highest demand. *Demand* is the number of visits to a service center multiplied by the average time taken for each visit. For example, if a workload is causing 100 disk accesses per second and the disk accesses takes 1 millisecond, then the demand for the disk is 100 milliseconds per second, or 10 percent. Following are concepts to keep in mind when analyzing bottlenecks.

- A *service center* is a resource in the system that tasks must wait for when the resource is servicing another task. The CPU, disks, controllers, and network are all examples of service centers. There can also be logical resources such as locks or critical sections in software. Memory is not a resource that a task waits for. If there is not enough memory, the system starts paging. Memory cannot be a bottleneck in itself. Rather, a shortage of memory can cause the disk subsystem to become a bottleneck.

- All bottlenecks are observed in the context of a workload. When a server is fulfilling a file-server role, its disks may be the source of the bottleneck. When the same server is acting as a domain controller, its CPU may be the bottleneck.

- For any combination of server and workload, there is a bottleneck. Usually the bottleneck resource is not overloaded in normal operation. When it is, a queue will build up in front of that resource and service times will climb. When this occurs, the source of the bottleneck must be relieved.

- There are two ways to relieve a bottleneck: You can decrease the visit rate to the resource (for example, by adding disks and spreading the load over them, thus decreasing the visit rate on each disk), or you can decrease the visit time, (for example, by installing faster disk drives on your computer). Keep in mind that one way to reduce the visit rate is to decrease the workload on the system, for example by moving some users to another server.

The figure below shows a characteristic respone time curve that all multiuser server share. As the load on the server increases, usage of the bottleneck resource comes closer to saturation (100 percent utilization) more of the time. As it does, there is more queuing in front of the resource and this causes response times to increase. As the resource nears 100 percent utilization, response times grow rapidly.

A server supporting happy users is not operating with its resources very close to saturation. There is some "elbow room" for the bottleneck resource, and the system operates in the part of the response curve that is below the acceptable response time limit. When the system is operating above that line, it's time to relieve the bottleneck.

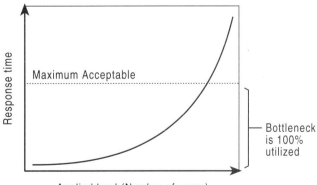

What Can Be Done About Bottlenecks?

When the server appears to have slow response times, you may install a faster processor without realizing that the disk subsystem is the actual bottleneck. In this case, you can improve response times somewhat because the disk is faster. However, the capacity of the system does not change; the bottleneck is the same.

The next figure illustrates what happens if you fail to identify the bottleneck correctly or if you improve the wrong resource. The capacity of the system does not change at all. At load levels approaching saturation of the bottleneck, users do not experience improved response times.

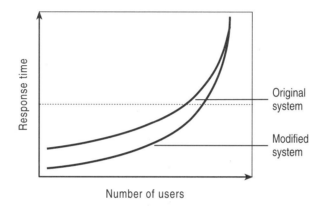

The figure below illustrates what happens when the bottleneck is correctly identified and relieved. Again, this is accomplished by decreasing the number of visits to the device or decreasing the time per visit. Not only are response times improved at light loads, but the saturation point moves farther out. Users experience acceptable response times at higher load levels. When you review this figure, note that there is a new bottleneck in the system, but hopefully the capacity is high enough to provide acceptable performance. If not, the new bottleneck must be found and resolved.

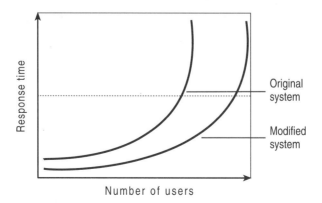

Impact of Memory and Cache

The server's memory and L2 cache (processor cache) generally cannot become bottlenecks. This is because they are not service centers; that is, processes don't wait for these resources. If there is insufficient memory in the system, it starts paging. This increases the visit rate on the disk, and the disk becomes the bottleneck. This is commonly known as *disk thrashing*. When you investigate a disk bottleneck, you must also examine the paging rate. For a Microsoft Exchange Server computer, if the paging rate is more than 100 pages per second, consider adding memory. Although memory isn't technically the bottleneck, adding memory can solve the problem by relieving the disk.

An inadequate L2 cache can cause the processors to stall while waiting for data from main memory. Excessive cache misses can cause the system bus to become a bottleneck. This is commonly known as *bus thrashing*, and is an element to watch for, especially in multiprocessor systems. If you believe this is happening in your server, you can install the Pentium counters available in the Windows NT Resource Kit compact disc and monitor bus utilization by using the Performance Monitor.

How to Monitor a Server

One of the most important elements of performance tuning is to maintain Performance Monitor logs. If you don't record this information, you will have nothing to work with. You can set these logs to record only every two or five minutes; this is sufficient for most performance tuning work and doesn't require too much storage space.

There are three major areas to watch when you are monitoring a server with live users.

Trends in submitted loads

Observe whether your users are sending more messages now than they did a few months ago, or whether the average message size is increasing. These factors will change the load on the server, and if you are not aware of them, the load can slowly increase until you have a response-time problem. Microsoft Exchange Server provides counters that give an indication of the overall workload.

Service times

If you monitor a server alone, it is nearly impossible to calculate the overall response times that users will experience. However, you can observe the server components of the response time, and get a general idea of whether slow server response times are becoming an issue. Microsoft Exchange Server provides counters that indicate server response times.

Resource use

By observing the utilization of various resources, you can see where the bottleneck in a system is and even get an idea of where the next bottleneck might occur, after relieving the current one.

The following sections describe the counters of most interest to an administrator, performance analyst, or capacity planner when performing system tuning.

Watching for Trends in the Load

These counters don't provide a complete picture of the load on your Microsoft Exchange Server computer, but they will indicate trends over time if you track them.

Object	Counter	Description
MSExchangeIS	User Count	The number of connected client sessions.
	Active User Count	The number of users who have been active in the last 10 minutes.
MSExchangeIS Private	Messages Submitted/min	The rate of messages being submitted to the private information store.
	Message Recipients Delivered/min	The rate of messages being delivered by the private information store. This will be higher than the submission rate because many messages have multiple recipients.
MSExchangeIS Public	Messages Submitted/min	The rate of messages being submitted to the public information store.
	Message Recipients Delivered/min	The rate of messages being delivered by the public information store. This will be higher than the submission rate because many messages have multiple recipients.
MSExchangeMTA	Messages/sec	The rate at which the MTA is processing messages.
	Messages Bytes/sec	The number of bytes in the messages being processed by the MTA. Divide this by the Messages/sec counter, and you can determine the average message size.

Watching Service Times

These counters don't provide a complete picture of the responsiveness of your Microsoft Exchange Server computer, but they will indicate trends over time if you track them.

Object	Counter	Description
MSExchangeIS Private	Send Queue Size	Indicates whether the information store is keeping up with the submitted load. The queue can be non-zero at peak traffic times, but it shouldn't stay there long after the peak has passed.
	Average Time for Delivery	Indicates how long it takes the information store to deliver messages.
MSExchangeIS Public	Send Queue Size	Indicates whether the information store is keeping up with the submitted load. The queue can be non-zero at peak traffic times, but it shouldn't stay there long after the peak has passed.
	Average Time for Delivery	Indicates how long it takes the information store to deliver messages.
MSExchangeMTA	Work Queue Length	Indicates whether the MTA is keeping up with the submitted load. The queue can be non-zero at peak traffic times, but it shouldn't stay there long after the peak has passed.

Processor Utilization

Windows NT provides additional counters that can help you analyze processor usage, but many are more useful to a developer than to an administrator. The following counters are relevant to bottleneck analysis.

Object	Counter
System	% Total Processor Time
Process	% Processor Time

If you observe processor utilization at a fine granularity, for example every one or five seconds, note that the counters fluctuate rapidly and will frequently hit 100 percent for short periods of time. For this reason, monitoring processor usage is more useful when averaged over a longer period of time. If you are monitoring for longer periods of time and you find that the processor usage reaches 100 percent and stays there for minutes or hours, your users are probably becoming impatient with response times. You may want to size your system for around 60 percent or 70 percent processor utilization during peak times, so that there is extra room for unexpected demands and for growth.

When you are running other services in addition to Microsoft Exchange Server on the server computer, it is recommended that you analyze per-process processor usage. This enables you to determine which services are using most of the CPU time, and how to appropriately balance the load.

If the processor is your bottleneck, consider taking the following actions:

Recommendations

- Use a faster processor or multiple processors.
- Use a larger L2 cache. This can improve processor efficiency.

Disk Counters

There are two sets of disk counters: LogicalDisk and PhysicalDisk. Either are fine to use, but LogicalDisk makes it easier to track drive usage. In either case, you must enable the disk counters. They are turned off by default, due to the small performance hit they create.

▶ **To enable Performance Monitor disk counters**

- At the command prompt, type **diskperf -y**. The counters take effect after the next reboot.

Following are important disk counters:

Object	Counter
LogicalDisk	Disk Bytes Written/sec
	Disk Bytes Read/sec
	Disk Reads/sec
	Disk Writes/sec
	Avg. Disk Queue Length
	% Disk Time (general indicator only; not a reliable indicator of disk saturation).

Compare the disk operations per second with the specifications for sustained operations provided by your vendor. If your disk operations per second are getting close to the vendor's specifications, you're nearing capacity. Note that the % Disk Time counter is not a fair indication of disk saturation. A disk that is busy 100 percent of the time may actually be capable of doing much more work, due to smart disk controllers and scheduling methods such as elevator algorithms.

Recommendations

If the disk subsystem is your bottleneck, consider taking the following actions:

- Use the fastest possible disks for the information store log and database.
- Use dedicated disks for the information store log.
- Stripe the information store database disks.
- Mirror the information store log; use RAID 5 on the information store database.
- Use high-performance controllers, and make sure that there are enough of them for your disks.
- Use a separate disk for MTA queues, or place these queues in the stripe set with the information store database.
- Use a separate disk for Internet Mail Service queues, or place these queues in the stripe set with the information store database.

Information Store Disk Demands

Object	Counter
MSExchangeDB	Buffer Asynchronous Reads/sec
	Buffer Asynchronous Writes/sec
	Buffer Synchronous Reads/sec
	Buffer Synchronous Writes/sec

Check the amount of disk activity generated by the information store. If you add up the read/write counters shown above, you can determine how much of the disk's activity on your information store database drive is due to the information store, and how much is generated by other services that might share the same drive.

Memory

Following are important memory counters:

Object	Counter
Memory	Pages/sec
	Page Faults/sec
	Available Bytes
	Committed Bytes
Process	Page Faults/sec
	Working Set

The Pages/sec counter indicates the rate at which pages are physically read or written on the paging drive. This indicates the contribution that paging makes to the demand for the disk.

The Page Faults/sec counter indicates the rate at which pages are faulted into the working sets of processes. Due to the page pool in the virtual memory system, the number of pages actually being read and written to disk is much less than the number of page faults. The page faults are of interest if you have services in addition to Microsoft Exchange Server running. In such a case, you can examine the rate of page faults on a per-process basis and determine where they are occurring. With this information, you can make application-tuning changes. For example, you might consider (carefully) adjusting the tradeoff between the information store buffer pool and the system memory pool. Also, by checking the per-process working sets, you can see identify the major memory allocations.

Recommendation

- If your paging rate is over a small amount, for example 100 pages/sec, consider adding memory.

The Available Bytes counter indicates how much physical memory is available at any given time. The system adjusts working sets of processes to keep this above a certain threshold, generally 4 MB. If this level is approached, you should see higher paging and page fault rates. The Committed Bytes counter indicates the amount of virtual address space that the system has committed to applications. This must be backed by the paging file on the disk, so make sure that there is space in the paging file.

Recommendation

- Anticipate memory issues by tracking trends in available and committed memory.

Buffers

Following are important buffer counters.

Object	Counter
MSExchangeDB	% Buffer Cache Hit
	Buffer Asynchronous Reads/sec
	Buffer Asynchronous Writes/sec
	Buffer Synchronous Reads/sec
	Buffer Synchronous Writes/sec

Depending on your usage patterns, you may be able optimize the use of server memory by adjusting the number of information store buffers. Monitor the % Buffer Cache Hit counter. If it is consistently very close to 100 percent, try decreasing the number of buffers. You should also monitor the information store disk activity. If the activity doesn't increase, your setting is correct. However, if you notice that the cache hit rate is less than 95 percent, try increasing the number of buffers. As long as the paging activity does not increase, the setting is correct. Be careful when making these changes! Make small adjustments and monitor the results until you're confident in the changes made.

Recommendations

- Consider adjusting your information store buffer usage if the cache hit rate is very high or low.

- If you cannot find a happy medium for this setting, you probably need to add more memory.

▶ **To change the number of information store buffers**

1. At the command prompt, type **PerfWiz -V**.

2. Change the setting number for the information store buffers, but be careful when doing this. Make small adjustments and monitor the results until you are confident with the changes made.

The Network Interface object can be obtained by installing the Windows NT Resource Kit. If your network connection is a point-to-point link, the counters below will show all traffic on the link. If the connection is a LAN, these counters will show the traffic to and from the server being monitored.

Object	Counter
Network Interface	Bytes Received/sec
	Bytes Sent/sec
	Packets Received/sec
	Packets Sent/sec

If you know the capacity ratings of your network and network interface card (NIC), you can compare these ratings to the values for the counters shown above and determine how close to capacity you are operating. For a more complete overview of network traffic, you can also use the Network Monitor tool available with Microsoft Systems Management Server (SMS). Note that Network Monitor is a stand-alone tool. You do not need to have other SMS components installed to run it.

If you find that the server is operating at or near network capacity, you can upgrade the network speed, for example, by moving from a 10-MB Ethernet to a 100-MB Ethernet, or moving from a 64-KB line to a T1 line. You may also want to consider using multiple Ethernet connections for the server, or multiple 64-KB lines, rather than one faster connection or line.

Recommendation

- Consider faster links, multiple interfaces, and multiple links.

System Bus

If you suspect that bus saturation is an issue that affects your server, you can monitor its activity on Pentium and Pentium Pro servers. Use the **p5ctrs** from the Windows NT Resource Kit. To view Pentium counters, you must run Pperf and then change the configuration.

Following are important bus counters:

Object	Counter
Pentium	Bus Utilization (clks)/sec
	% Code Cache Misses
	% Data Cache Misses

If your system bus is near saturation, you have two options:

- If there are many cache misses, you can use larger CPU caches; or
- You can split the load onto multiple servers. Start by offloading any non-Microsoft Exchange Server services, if they are being used.

Recommendations

- Use larger L2 caches.
- Consider multiple servers.

C H A P T E R   4

Microsoft Exchange Server Disaster Recovery

This chapter describes techniques that can be used for Microsoft Exchange Server disaster recovery planning. For quick answers to many frequently asked questions, see the "Disaster Recovery Frequently Asked Questions" section.

Before reading this chapter, read Chapter 15 of the *Microsoft Exchange Server Administrator's Guide*. Although Microsoft Exchange Server is a robust and stable messaging platform, it is essential that you have a working plan to restore Microsoft Exchange Server computers and data in a timely way if a system crash or another disaster occurs. By reading this chapter, you can minimize downtime for your organization and provide the quickest possible data recovery. However, it is important that you do not take this information for granted. Instead, test, formulate, and certify your own disaster recovery plans.

Because Microsoft Exchange uses Windows NT® security for authentication, you must also consider Windows NT operating system backup and restoration procedures, as well as procedures for Microsoft Exchange Server backup and restoration. Due to this relationship, Microsoft Exchange Server disaster recovery cannot be considered independently from Windows NT disaster recovery.

An enhanced version of the Windows NT Ntbackup.exe program is available on the Microsoft Exchange Server compact disc. One of the benefits of Microsoft Exchange Server and the new Ntbackup.exe program is that they provide live backup of the Microsoft Exchange information store and directory without causing interruption to the messaging system. Ntbackup.exe also provides file-based backup services that back up the Windows NT registry.

The following figure shows the updated Ntbackup.exe program with Microsoft Exchange Server extensions.

Microsoft Exchange Server does not need to be taken offline to perform backup. The entire information store, directory, message transfer agent (MTA), and system attendant remain in service during online backup. Although the information store and directory can be backed up online, files in directories being accessed by other Microsoft Exchange Server for Windows NT services, such as the DX or PCMTA services [Microsoft Mail Connector (Appletalk) MTA], should be backed up when the respective service is not running. You can automate and schedule this backup by using the Winat.exe graphical user interface (GUI) scheduler. For more information, see the *Windows NT Resource Kit*. An example of a batch file that shuts down and restarts Microsoft Exchange Server services is also discussed in this chapter. This batch file can be used for other purposes as well.

Defining Data to Back Up

Two types of data must be backed up: user data and configuration data. Microsoft Exchange Server *user data* is stored in the public information store and the private information store (Pub.edb, Priv.edb), personal folder files (.psts), offline folder files (.osts), personal address books (.pabs), and transaction logs. Microsoft Exchange Server configuration data is stored in the Microsoft Exchange Server directory (Dir.edb), the Windows NT registry, and in various subdirectories in the Microsoft Exchange Server installation path (and potentially in paths created after you run the Microsoft Exchange Performance Optimizer). Depending on the type of backup and restoration required, these data points must be considered in your procedures.

The Microsoft Exchange Server database files are located in the directories listed in the table below. Although the default path of Exchsrvr is used in this table, you can change the location of the database files at the time of installation. To place the transaction logs on a separate physical disk from the information store and directory files, run the Microsoft Exchange Server Performance Optimizer. You can also reconfigure the paths for all database files by using the **Database Paths** tab for the server object.

Data	Path Name
Private information store	Exchsrvr\Mdbdata\Priv.edb
Public information store	Exchsrvr\Mdbdata\Pub.edb
Directory	Exchsrvr\Dsadata\Dir.edb
Information store transaction logs	Exchsrvr\Mdbdata*.log

Backing Up .Pst, .Ost, and .Pab Files

The .pst, .ost, and .pab files are specific to each user within a Microsoft Exchange Server organization. Below are descriptions for each file type and suggestions for using and storing these files. For more information on data recovery procedures specific to each of these file types, see the ".Pst, .Ost, and .Pab Recovery" section.

.Pst Files

If users store .pst files on their local drives, and local drives are not being backed up, you cannot restore these files. If .pst files are stored on a file server, you need to include them in your backup routine. You can restore a .pst, and then add it to an existing user profile. If a user has password protected his or her .pst file and then forgets the password, you cannot recover the password or the data in that file. Make sure that your users are aware of this. You can repair a damaged .pst file, however, by running the Inbox Repair Tool (Scanpst.exe). For more information, see the "Using the Inbox Repair Tool to Repair .Pst and .Ost Files" section.

.Ost Files

Data in .ost files is at risk when changes have been made to the local .ost file and have not yet been replicated to the server-based store. If a user's computer fails, a new .ost file can be created on the replacement computer and all server-based information can be sent to the .ost file through synchronization. You can repair a damaged .ost file by running the Inbox Repair Tool. For more information, see the "Using the Inbox Repair Tool to Repair .Pst and .Ost Files" section.

.Pab Files

Personal address book files can be stored on a server directory or locally. Because most servers are backed up regularly at night, any server-based .pab files are also backed up. A .pab file may be lost when a user stores it locally and do not arrange for a backup. If the .pab entries must be replaced, this can cost an employee many hours of work and lost productivity.

Archiving and AutoArchiving Data with Microsoft Outlook

You can use Microsoft Outlook™ to archive data into .pst files automatically. If you plan to use this feature, make sure that you consider archive data files when planning backup strategies.

Your Outlook mailbox grows when items are created in the same way that papers pile up on your desk. In the paper-based world, you can occasionally shuffle through all your documents and archive important but not frequently used files. Documents that are less important, such as newspapers and magazines, you can discard.

When working in Outlook, you can transfer old items to a storage file manually by choosing **Archive** from the **File** menu, or you can transfer or delete old items automatically by using the AutoArchive feature. Items are considered old when they reach the age you specify.

Note Outlook can archive only files that are stored in a mail folder, such as an attached Microsoft Excel spreadsheet or Microsoft Word document. A file that is not stored in a mail folder cannot be archived.

▶ **To start AutoArchive**

Running AutoArchive is a simple two-step process.

1. In Microsoft Outlook, from the **Tools** menu, choose **Options**.
2. Select **AutoArchive**.

Setting AutoArchive Properties

You must set the AutoArchive properties for each folder you want archived. You can also choose when to archive these folders. Individual folders, groups of folders, or all Outlook folders can be archived automatically. The process runs automatically whenever you start Outlook. AutoArchive checks the date of the items you specify and moves old items to your archive file. Items in the Deleted Items folder are not moved to another folder. They are deleted.

Several Outlook folders are created after you select AutoArchive. These folders and their default *aging periods* (the default time by which an item is considered old) are as follows:

- Calendar (six months)
- Tasks (six months)
- Journal (six months)
- Sent Items (two months)
- Deleted Items (two months)

Note that AutoArchive does not archive the Inbox, Notes, and Contacts folders automatically.

Exporting and Archiving

There is a difference between exporting and archiving. When you *archive*, the original items are copied to the archive file and then removed from the current folder. When you *export*, the original items are copied to the export file but are not removed from the current folder. In addition, you can only archive to one file type, a personal folder file, but you can export to many file types such as text.

When you archive, your existing folder structure is maintained in your new archive file. If there is a parent folder above the folder you choose to archive, the parent folder is created in the archive file, but items within the parent folder are not archived in the archive file. In this way, an identical folder structure exists between the archive file and your mailbox. Folders are left in place after being archived, even if they are empty.

Backup Types

To help you establish a backup strategy, this section reviews backup types and provides a better understanding of online and offline backups.

Online Backups Versus Offline Backups

Microsoft Exchange Server *online backups* require that the respective service (information store or directory) is running. These backups do not disrupt messaging on Microsoft Exchange Server computers. Note that you can back up the directory service without the information store running. You can also include the Windows NT registry in the backup job.

An *offline backup* is a file-based backup. Unlike online backups, offline backups require that all Microsoft Exchange Server services be stopped. After you stop these services, you can run the Windows NT NTbackup program to back up all files on the desired drives.

Online Backup Types

An online backup is comprised of the following four types of backups:

Normal (Full)

In a *normal backup*, the entire information store and directory databases are backed up. Transaction logs are backed up and then purged. Incremental and differential backups are given context as a result of the transaction logs being purged.

Copy

A *copy backup* is similar to a full backup, except there is no context marking. The context for the incremental and differential backups does not get changed. Log files are not deleted. A copy backup is analogous to taking a snapshot of the databases at a given point in time without impacting other backup routines. You can use a copy backup to reproduce a particular scenario in a test environment.

Incremental

In an *incremental backup*, only a subset of the information store and/or directory is backed up. Only changes since the last full or incremental backup (whichever was most recent), are written to tape. Only the .log files are written to tape. These files are then purged. The purging of transaction logs sets the context for the next backup job.

For a typical incremental backup, a tape of the last full backup is required, as well as tapes for each incremental restore up to the point when the system experienced an outage. For example, a full backup can be performed on Sunday evening, while incremental backups are performed on a daily basis from Monday through Friday. If an outage occurs on Friday morning, a full backup can be performed and each incremental backup tape can be restored through Thursday. Services should not be started until the final incremental tape has been restored. Note that an incremental backup is disabled when circular logging is enabled.

Differential

A *differential backup* backs up the changes in the information store and/or directory since the last full (normal) or incremental backup. However, most administrators do not mix differential and incremental backups in a series. Only .log files are backed up, but they are not purged from disk. For example, if a transaction log and database restore are required, only two tapes are required for the differential backup. The two required tapes would be the latest full backup and the latest differential backup. Note that differential backup is disabled when circular logging is enabled.

If the transaction logs are intact since the last full backup, only the last full backup tape is required. This is because the restore process plays back all logs from the point of the last full backup to the current Edb.log file, thus restoring all transactions to date.

Caution   When restoring data, make sure that you do not select **Erase existing data**; otherwise, you'll erase the log files to date.

Log Files and Circular Logging

Although transparent to the end user, Microsoft Exchange Server maintains several database files or stores. The information store consists of two databases: the private information store (Priv.edb) and public information store (Pub.edb). The Microsoft Exchange Server directory is stored in the Dir.edb file. The respective Microsoft Exchange Server services use transaction log files for each of these databases. The information store service manages both the public and private information store databases.

Microsoft Exchange Server implements log files to accept, track, and maintain data. All message transactions are written first to log files and memory, and then to their respective database files. This is done to optimize performance and recoverability.

Because log files are written to sequentially and Microsoft Exchange Server writes message transactions to log files immediately, Microsoft Exchange Clients experience a high level of performance. Log files are always appended to the end of the file. However, Microsoft Exchange Server database files are written to randomly.

To optimize recoverability, log files can be used to recover message transaction data if a hardware failure corrupts the information store or directory database files, provided you have backed up the logs or the logs are intact. Log files are typically maintained on a separate physical disk drive from the information store and directory database files.

If database files are damaged, a backup can be restored and any data that has not been backed up but has been recorded in the transaction logs, can be played back. These transactions are entered into the restored database file to bring the database up-to-date.

The directory and information store services use the following logs and files:

- Transaction logs
- Previous logs
- Checkpoint files
- Reserved logs
- Patch files

Transaction Logs

Transaction logs can be kept on a separate physical drive from that of their respective .edb files. By default, information store logs are maintained in the Exchsrvr\Mdbdata directory and directory service logs are maintained in Exchsrvr\Dsadata.

Each subdirectory contains an Edb.log file, which is the current transaction log file for the respective service. Both the information store subdirectory and the directory service subdirectories maintain a separate Edb.log file. Log files should always be 5,242,880 bytes in size. If log files are not this size, they are probably damaged.

Because transactions are first written to the Edb.log files and then written to the database, the current actual or effective database is a combination of the uncommitted transactions in the transaction log file, which also reside in memory, and the actual .edb database file.

When the Edb.log files are filled with transaction data, they are renamed and a new Edb.log file is created. Note that .log files are always 5 MB, regardless of how many transactions have been recorded in them.

Previous Logs

When an Edb.log is renamed, the renamed log files are stored in the same subdirectory as the Edb.log file. The log files are named in a sequential numbering order (for example, Edb00014.log, Edb00015.log, and so on). Note that hexadecimal numbers are used.

Previously committed log files are purged by the Windows NT Ntbackup.exe program during an online normal (full) backup or an online incremental backup. However, not all previous log files are purged. After every 5 MB of transactions are written, a new log is created, but not necessarily committed. There may be several previous .log files that aren't committed that will not be purged.

When circular logging is enabled, a history of previous .log files is not maintained and therefore these .log files are not purged by backup operations. In fact, incremental and differential online backups are not permitted when circular logging is enabled. Note that transactions in log files are committed to the respective .edb file when the service is shut down normally. For example, when the information store service experiences a normal shutdown (that is, the service shuts down with no errors), any transactions that existed in log files and not in Priv.Edb and/or Pub.Edb files are committed to the .edb files. Note that .log files should not be manually purged while services are running. In general, it is best to purge logs by using the backup process.

Checkpoint Files

Checkpoint files are used for recovering data from transaction logs into .edb files. The *checkpoint* is the place marker within the Edb.chk file that indicates which transactions have been committed. Separate Edb.chk files are maintained by the information store and directory services. Whenever data is written to an .edb file from the transaction log, the Edb.chk file is updated with information specifying that the transaction was successfully committed to the respective .edb file.

During the data recovery process, Microsoft Exchange Server determines which transactions have not yet been committed to the respective .edb file by reading the Edb.chk file or by reading the transaction log files directly. Note that the Edb.chk file is not required.

The information store and directory service each reads its Edb.chk file during startup. Any transactions that have not been committed are restored into the .edb files from transaction logs. For example, if a Microsoft Exchange Server computer experiences an outage, and transactions have been recorded into the transaction log but not yet to the actual database file, Microsoft Exchange Server attempts to recover this data on startup by recording transactions from the logs to the respective database files automatically.

Reserved Logs

The directory and information store services independently maintain two reserve files: Res1.log and Res2.log. These files are stored in the Mdbdata and Dsadata directories. If the directory and/or information store service is renaming the Edb.log file and attempting to create a new Edb.log file, and there is not enough disk space to create a new Edb.log file, the reserve log files are used. This is a fail-safe mechanism that is only used in the event of an emergency. When this occurs, an error message is sent to the respective service. The service will flush any transactions in memory that have not yet been written to a transaction log into the Res1.log file, and if necessary, the Res2.log file. When this is completed, the service shuts down and records an event in the Windows NT EventLog. Note that RES (reserve) transaction log files are always 5 MB in size, the same as all transaction log files.

Patch Files

The patch file mechanism was designed for the situation where transactions are written to a database during the backup process. A convenient feature of Microsoft Exchange Server is the ability to back up databases without interrupting service to end users. During the backup operation, data is read from the .edb files.

If a transaction is made to a section of the .edb file that has already been backed up, it is recorded in a .pat (patch) file. If a transaction is made to a section of the .edb file that has not yet been backed up, it is processed and does not need to be written to the patch file. A separate .pat file is used for each database: Priv.pat, Pub.pat, and Dir.pat. Note that these .pat files will only be exposed during the backup process. During an online backup operation, the following occurs:

1. A .pat file is created for the current database.
2. The backup operation for the current .edb file begins.
3. Transactions that must be written to sections of the .edb file that have already been backed up are recorded to the .edb file and the .pat file.
4. The .pat file is written to the backup tape.
5. The .pat file is deleted from the Mdbdata or Dsadata directory.

Temp.edb File

The Temp.edb file is used to store transactions that are in progress. Temp.Edb is also used for some transient storage during online compaction.

Purging Log Files

When circular logging is disabled, log files accumulate on the transaction log disk drive until an online normal (full) or incremental backup is performed. During an online backup operation, the following occurs:

1. The backup process copies the specified database files.
2. Patch files are created as required (patch files maintain transactions written during a backup operation to the portion of an .edb file that has already been backed up).
3. Log files created during the backup process are copied to tape.
4. Patch files are written to tape.
5. Log files older than the checkpoint at the start of the backup operation are purged. These files are not required because the transactions have already been committed to the .edb files and the .edb files have been written to tape.

Database Circular Logging

Database circular logging uses transaction log technology but does not maintain previous transaction log files. Instead, a few log files are maintained and eventually purged as new log files are created. When transactions in transaction log files have been committed to the database, the existing log files are removed and previous transactions are discarded by this process. Circular logging is enabled by default. Although circular logging helps manage disk space and prevents the buildup of transaction log files, differential and incremental backups cannot be performed because these backups rely on past transaction log files.

When database circular logging is enabled, you may see multiple Edbxxxxx.log files in the Mdbdata or Dsadata directories. This is normal, because Microsoft Exchange Server uses several log files before setting the circular window (wrapping around). For example, the Edb00010.log, Edb00011.log, Edb00012.log, and Edb00013.log files would become Edb00011.log, Edb00012.l log, Edb00013.log, and Edb00014.log.

Microsoft Exchange Server attempts to maintain a window of four log files for circular logging. However, if the server I/O load is large, more than four log files will be used. Log files in excess of four will not be purged until the respective service (information store and/or directory service) is stopped and then restarted.

Verifying That Circular Logging Is Enabled

To verify whether database circular logging settings are enabled, perform the following steps:

1. In the Microsoft Exchange Server Administrator program, choose a server, and then select **Configuration**.
2. From the **File** menu, choose **Properties**.
3. Select the **Advanced** tab.
4. View the circular logging settings.

Circular logging can be set separately for the information store and directory, and you can change these settings at any time by using the Administrator program. However, Microsoft Exchange Server will stop the corresponding service and restart it after making changes.

Transaction Logs Recovery

The following example describes how transaction logs are recovered.

The circumstances are as follows:

- Circular logging is not enabled
- The transaction logs are stored on a disk separate from the database files.
- The last full (normal) backup took place two days ago.
- Due to a hardware failure, such as a bad hard disk, the information store databases become damaged, but the transaction log drive remains intact.

Do the above circumstances dictate that the best you can do is lose two days of production data? The answer is no. Because the transaction logs are complete, they contain all transactions from the point of the last full backup.

In this case, after the hardware is restored, you need to perform a full restore. Do not select **Erase All Existing Data**, which prompts the backup program to remove all existing log files. The full restore writes the database files and the log files that were backed up with the last full backup.

The restored log files are any log file saved up to the first log file on the current transaction log drive. For example, suppose that the full backup copied Edb00012.log through Edb00014.log. The log files on the transaction log drive would be Edb00015.log and up. The full restore will copy Edb00012.log through Edb00014.log and the information store database files that are part of the backup set.

When the information store service is started, it restores transactions from Edb00012.log through the last log file (such as Edb00019.log) and Edb.log, the most recent log file. After this is completed, the database will be up-to-date. The log files contain signatures, which ensure that these files are included in the sequence to be restored.

Transaction Characteristics

Atomicity

Results of the transaction's execution are either all committed or all rolled back.

In Microsoft Exchange Server, atomic operations are achieved through the use of transaction logs. As mentioned earlier, transactions in the log that haven't yet been committed to the main database file are either rolled forward and committed, or are rolled back if incomplete. This process happens quickly and automatically when the system is restarted.

Consistency

A shared resource (such as a database) is always transformed from one valid state to another valid state. All operations on the Microsoft Exchange Server information store are atomic, and ensure that the data is always in a consistent state. Updating a transaction log to indicate that a transaction has been completely committed back to the main database file is an atomic operation.

Isolation

Transactions are recorded in a serial fashion in a system handling multiple simultaneous transactions. The result of any transaction is the same as if it were the only transaction running on the system. This implies that safe, concurrent access to the data by multiple simultaneous users occurs. Simultaneous user operations cannot interfere with each other in a way that renders the database invalid. The isolation property is enforced by the database underlying the Microsoft Exchange Server information store.

Durability

The results of a transaction are permanent and survive future system and media failures. Microsoft Exchange Server transaction logs implement the principle of *durability*. If, for example, a portion of a log file is corrupt or unreadable due to physical drive damage, those transactions are rolled back.

Even with media damage, the physical format of transaction logs is carefully designed to reduce the impact of any media failure, through a combination of sequential writes, the creation of new log files every 5 MB, and low-level techniques logging. This last technique maximizes the durability of transactions, even within a partially corrupted log file.

Concern has been expressed that using transaction logs can incur significant overhead because the data must be written more than once (first to the log, then to the main database file). However, the correct use of transaction logs actually *improves* overall system throughput, for a number of reasons.

When transaction log files are stored on a separate disk, they are written sequentially, rather than through random access. Because the disk drive head doesn't have to seek randomly, the process is faster than random-access writes to the main database file (even with today's fast hard drive subsystems). The transaction log files are then "lazily" committed back to the main database file. (Lazy commit is similar to lazy write, which is the ability to record changes in the file structure cache, which is quicker than recording them on disk, and then later, when demand on the computer's central processing unit (CPU) is low, the Cache Manager writes the changes to the disk.) This can be accomplished efficiently for the following reasons:

- The transactions are processed asynchronously, when the server has idle cycles.
- The Windows NT file system (NTFS) and file allocation table (FAT) disk cache systems in Windows NT Server automatically order the writes in the most efficient manner, through classic techniques, to minimize physical head seeks.

In addition, Microsoft Exchange Server recovery techniques work as well for large records as they do for small ones. This is because the transaction logs are smart enough to write only the data that has actually changed. Therefore, if a user changes only a few bytes of a 2-MB document stored in a Microsoft Exchange Server computer, only the actual data pages that are changed are written to the log.

Automatic Recovery Using Transaction Rollback

When the Microsoft Exchange Server information store or directory services is started after abnormal server shutdown, the transaction log file is scanned for incomplete transactions. If incomplete transactions exist, they are rolled back automatically to the state in which they existed before the transaction took place. This automatic recovery operation occurs relatively quickly, because only the most recent transactions in the log must be checked.

Single-instance Storage with Automatic Referential Integrity

Single-instance storage is a key requirement from customers who want to store users' mail centrally, on the server. With single-instance storage, if 100 users on the same server all receive the same message, only a single copy of the message is stored on the server, and 100 pointers to the message are placed in the users' mailboxes. Significant space savings and server performance gains can be realized with single-instance storage.

Microsoft Exchange Server has built single-instance storage capabilities into its information store design from the ground up, as opposed to stringing together existing databases. Single-instance storage is always in effect; it requires no special configuration or administration, and most important, it is intrinsic to the information store. When a message or user mailbox is deleted, the correct thing always happens; messages cannot be orphaned or lost. Pointers cannot get out of sync between files because everything is stored in a single file, and referential integrity is handled internally by the database engine.

Single-Instance Storage with Per-User Storage Limits

With Microsoft Exchange Server, you are given control of storage. Research shows that one of the most common reasons for mail system outages is the inability to limit user storage, which eventually causes servers to fill up and cease working. Therefore, within its shared mail information store, Microsoft Exchange Server enables administrators to set and enforce disk quotas, either as an overall default, or as individual user limits.

Users can be given a warning limit as well as a fixed limit. The fixed limit is enforced by prohibiting the offending user from sending any new e-mail until the user cleans up his or her mailbox. In this way, this user will not miss any critical incoming e-mail messages, and other users won't receive non-delivery notices from the offending user's mailbox.

Online Backups to Tape

Microsoft Exchange Server includes built-in support for running online backups directly to tape media. The server does not have to be shut down, nor do users have to be logged off. Furthermore, Microsoft Exchange Server backup is integrated with Windows NT Server backup, which enables you to back up both Microsoft Exchange Server computers and file servers from the same location. You can perform full, incremental, or differential backups directly to a wide variety of tape devices, from ¼ inch cartridges to high-capacity digital audio tape (DAT) systems.

Examples of Data Recovery

Procedures for the following data recovery scenarios are discussed in this section:

- Single mailbox recovery
- Full server recovery
- .Pst, .ost, and .pab file recovery

Single Mailbox Recovery

Data recovery for a single mailbox may be necessary in the event of an accidental mailbox or mailbox data deletion. In a centrally supported organization, affiliate offices can mail tapes to an internal recovery center.

Instructions for data recovery for a single mailbox are described in this section. These procedures will enable single mailbox recovery for any server in your organization, regardless of the server name.

Before trying any of the example procedures, note the following.

Caution   This procedure should not be performed on a server that is in production. As noted below, this procedure requires restoring data to a server that is not part of your production Microsoft Exchange Server site. The dedicated recovery server is installed using the same site and organization name as the production site; however, it is installed by selecting Create New Site.

The following components are required to create this example:

- A dedicated server with enough capacity to restore the entire private information store database.
- A backup of the private information store database.
- Microsoft Exchange Client and Microsoft Exchange Server installation code.
- Windows NT and the latest Windows NT Service Pack installation code.

Note   You must restore the entire information store and then retrieve data from the desired mailbox. You can prepare a server running Windows NT Server and then install Microsoft Exchange Server with the same site and organization name in which the mailbox to be restored resided. Then, restore the information store from a backup tape, log on with Microsoft Exchange Administrator privileges, and assign the Windows NT Administrator ID access to the desired mailbox. Restore mailbox data to a .pst file and then attach the .pst to the desired user profile.

Preparing the Non-Production Recovery Computer

For the fastest recovery, the non-production computer should be running and available for recovery at all times. This computer can be installed as a Windows NT primary domain controller (PDC), backup domain controller (BDC), or member server. The server should also have the appropriate Windows NT Service Pack installed.

Before recovering the data, make sure there is enough disk space for restoring the entire information store from your backup tape. The backup recovery computer should also be equipped with a tape drive that is compatible with the tape drives deployed on production servers. The tape drive should be tested and known to be working at all times.

During the installation of Microsoft Exchange Server, do not join the site. The recovery computer should be a stand-alone computer and should not be joined with your existing production site.

The Process

Log on to Windows NT as an administrator and install Microsoft Exchange Server (using the Complete installation option). Use the same site and organization name that was used on the server from which you are restoring the mailbox. Do not join the site. Note that the server name of the restore computer does not matter for the single mailbox restore procedure. This is because you are only restoring the information store, not the directory.

If you have a dedicated recovery server at each location, you can install Microsoft Exchange Server before starting the recovery. If the recovery server will be shared among sites, it is best to keep a copy of the Microsoft Exchange installation code on the hard drive for quick installation, so you can install Microsoft Exchange Server based on the required site and organization. The paths for this Microsoft Exchange Server installation do not need to match the paths of the production Microsoft Exchange Server installation being recovered.

After you complete the preceding steps, you can install the Microsoft Exchange Client on the recovery server.

Restoring the Information Store from Tape

This procedure assumes that a tape from an online backup is used for the restore. If an offline tape is used, do not choose to start the services after the restore. The following steps describe how to restore the information store from tape.

▶ **To restore the information store from tape**

1. Insert the backup tape and log on to the recovery domain as an administrator.

2. From the **Administrative Tools** program group, run BACKUP.

3. From the **Operations** menu, choose **Microsoft Exchange**.

4. Select the tapes icon, and then double-click the tape name.

5. In the right pane of the Tapes window, choose **Org**, **Site**, **Server**, **Information Store**.

6. Choose **Restore** from the upper part of the Backup menu's main screen.

7. In the Restore Information window, type the name of the destination server in the **Destination Server** box.

8. Select **Erase All Existing Data**, **Private**, **Public**, **Verify After Restore**, **Start Service After Restore**, and then choose **OK**. After you choose OK, the following message appears:

   "You are about to restore Microsoft Exchange components. The Microsoft Exchange services on the destination server will be stopped."

9. Choose **OK**.

10. In the Verify Status window, choose **OK**.

11. After the restore is completed, start the Directory Service service.

12. At the command prompt, switch to the Exchsrvr\Bin directory, and type

    isinteg –patch

    This will run the ISINTEG troubleshooting utility in patch mode. After you run ISINTEG, a message appears stating that the databases have been successfully updated. Now you can start the Microsoft Exchange Server information store and the other services.

13. In Control Panel, double-click the **Services** icon, and then verify that the relevant Microsoft Exchange Server services are running.

Recovering a User's Mailbox

Follow the steps described below to recover a user's mailbox.

▶ **To recover a user's mailbox**

1. Log on to the recovery server using the Windows NT Administrator ID.

2. In the Administrator window, choose **Servers**, and then select a server.

3. From the **File** menu, choose **Properties**.

4. Select the **Advanced** tab.

5. Under **DS/IS consistency adjustment**, select **All Inconsistencies**.

6. Choose **Adjust**.

7. Select **Recipients**, and then double-click a user's mailbox name.

8. Select the **General** tab, and then select **Primary Windows NT Account**.

9. Choose **Select An Existing Windows NT Account**, and then choose **OK**.

10. In the **Add User** box, select **Administrator**, and then choose **Add**.

11. In the **User Property** window, choose **OK**.

12. In the Microsoft Exchange Client, start the Microsoft Exchange services.

13. Configure a profile for the appropriate user.

14. Add a .pst file to the profile.

15. Restart the Microsoft Exchange Client.

16. In the left pane, select **Mailbox - Username**.

17. Select the first folder or item in the list on the right pane.

18. From the **Edit menu**, choose **Select All**.

19. From the **File menu**, choose **Copy**.

20. In the **Copy** dialog box, select the appropriate .pst file, and then choose **OK**. All data will be copied to this .pst file.

21. Copy the .pst file to the destination location.

22. Add this .pst file to the user's profile on the production server or send the .pst file to the user with instructions.

If you have network access, you can copy the recovered .pst file to the appropriate server.

The following figure illustrates the Microsoft Exchange Server single mailbox recovery process.

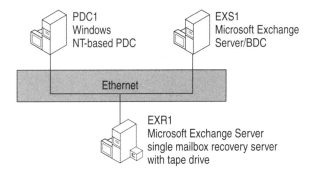

The single mailbox recovery server can be maintained online with production servers because the server name does not need to be the same as the production server running Microsoft Exchange Server. This recovery server, however, should not perform directory service replication with the production servers.

The following figure illustrates a topology for maintaining a spare server for single mailbox recovery. Note that the spare server "Sabc" is not joined to the production site. However, the server was installed using the same site name and organization name as the production site.

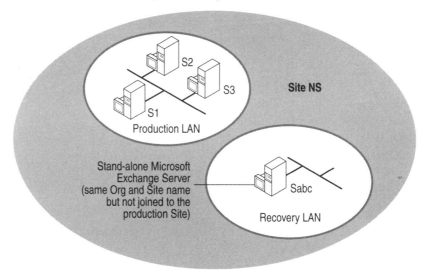

Organization Ferguson & Bardell

Full Server Recovery

You can *restore data* from one full Microsoft Exchange Server to a different computer, and you can also *move* Microsoft Exchange Server data from one computer to a new computer. This section describes how to restore data from one Microsoft Exchange Server computer to a different computer.

A full server recover is a special case because Windows NT is reinstalled and a new registry is created. In this situation, a new Windows NT security identifier (SID) must be created for the recovery computer in the domain, as outlined below.

Note The information in this section is also useful for moving a Microsoft Exchange Server installation to a more powerful server for a hardware upgrade. Keep in mind that the Windows NT registry can be restored to the same physical computer. This may be useful when a hard drive is being replaced on the same computer. In this case, if you restore the Windows NT registry, the computer maintains its unique SID, so you do not need to create a new SID by using the procedures below.

In addition to performing a full restore of the Microsoft Exchange Server databases (information store/directory service), it may also be necessary to restore the Windows NT Security Accounts Manager (SAM) database. Microsoft Exchange Server automatically adds two accounts upon initial installation: the Windows NT service account and the Windows NT account that were logged on to during the initial installation of the software. Although both accounts receive special privileges during installation, to restore the Microsoft Exchange Server directory service, you only need the Windows NT account SID that was originally used during the installation. The Microsoft Exchange directory service will not be accessible unless this SID exists in the Windows NT environment. If no domain controllers of the original domain are available, you must restore the Windows NT primary domain controller SAM.

Following are the requirements for a full server recovery.

- A full backup of the information store and directory.
- A replacement computer with the same hardware capacity as the production server.
- Access to the original Windows NT SAM.
- Production server configuration sheet.
- Microsoft Exchange Server installation code.
- Windows NT Server and the latest Windows NT Service Pack installation code.
- Microsoft Exchange Production Server configuration sheet.

A full server recovery is more complex than a single mailbox recovery. A *full server recovery* is defined as the ability to restore an original production Microsoft Exchange Server such that all Windows NT security and configuration information is recovered, as well as Microsoft Exchange Server configuration information and other data. A full server recovery enables users to use their current passwords to log on to their mailboxes when a recovery server is deployed.

Where a single mailbox recovery requires that only the information store be restored, a full server recovery requires that both the information store and directory service be restored. Microsoft Exchange Server relies on Windows NT security for providing access to mailbox data. Microsoft Exchange Server uses Windows NT account SID information in object properties within the Microsoft Exchange Server directory.

For a successful directory service recovery, two key conditions must be met:

- The directory service must be restored to a Windows NT Server computer that has the same site, organization, and server name as the production server.
- The recovery server must have access from the domain in which Microsoft Exchange Server was originally installed.

A full-server disaster recovery involves three computers. Two computers will be in production; one is a non-production or non-essential computer (meaning that such a computer can be in production performing some other task, but will be available at any time for recovery). One computer is a PDC. A second computer, usually a Microsoft Exchange Server computer, is configured as a BDC. The third computer is designated as a recovery server.

The requirement for a configuration that incorporates a PDC, BDC, and recovery server is due to the way in which Microsoft Exchange Server uses the Windows NT SAM database to provide authentication to directory objects. A full-server restore including the information store and directory requires access to the SAM from the domain in which the Microsoft Exchange Server computer was first installed.

For example, if you have one Microsoft Exchange Server computer in a site, and this server also acts as a PDC, you can have a recovery server offline. The Microsoft Exchange information store and directory are backed up nightly. If this server fails, a backup PDC with Microsoft Exchange Server can be built from scratch and the information store can be restored. When the Microsoft Exchange Server directory is restored, it expects the security properties of all directory objects to match the Windows NT SAM for the respective accounts.

Caution Because the backup computer was rebuilt as a PDC, a new Windows NT SAM is created. The restored Microsoft Exchange directory objects will not match the SAM objects, you will not be able to log on to the Microsoft Exchange Server Administrator program, and the Microsoft Exchange Server services will not be able to start. All restored data will be inaccessible if the Microsoft Exchange directory is restored in this case. Although you can restore the information store without the directory to access the data for each mailbox, this will only provide administrator access to mailbox data, and it is not considered full server recovery. The original Microsoft Exchange Server directory information will be lost from the production server.

As an example, suppose that there is a dedicated PDC, a production Microsoft Exchange Server computer that acts as a BDC, and a recovery server. The production Microsoft Exchange Server computer fails. You can build a Windows NT domain controller from the recovery server with the same computer name as the Microsoft Exchange Server computer that failed.

You can connect this to the domain as a BDC, which provides you with a copy of the SAM from the domain in which the production Microsoft Exchange Server computer resided. Using Server Manager, you first delete the original computer name, the BDC definition, from the PDC. Add it again during the BDC installation.

This procedure is necessary because each computer name receives a unique SID when it is added to the domain, and you will need a new SID for the recovery computer. After you have done this, install Microsoft Exchange Server using the same site and organization name. By default, the same server name will be used because Microsoft Exchange Server uses the computer name to create the Microsoft Exchange Server name. If you are recovering a server and joining an existing site during this reinstallation, see the *Microsoft Exchange Server Administrator's Guide*.

Creating a New SID for the Recovery Server

1. Install Microsoft Exchange Server on the new or repaired server, but do not replicate it with the existing organization.
2. Give the server its original organization and site name.
3. Run Setup. Do not join an existing site.
4. Create a new site with the same organization and site name.
5. After Setup is complete, upgrade the recovery server to the same Microsoft Exchange Service Pack as the production server.

Now you can restore the information store and directory from the last Microsoft Exchange Server production computer. Note that you could have added the recovery server to the production domain as a member server instead of a BDC.

Using a Backup Tape of the Information Store and Directory Service for a Server Recovery

The following is an example of a server recovery using a backup tape of the production server information store and directory service. Note that a normal (full) online backup of the information store and directory was performed. During the Microsoft Exchange Server software installation, do not join the site. Instead, select **Create New Site**. This is because you have a backup copy of the Microsoft Exchange Server directory database. Even though you chosen to create a new site, when you restart the server, it will synchronize automatically with other servers in the site because the knowledge of being in a site is stored in the directory database.

Preparing the Recovery Computer

When you prepare the recovery computer, note that you need to install Windows NT with the same computer name as the Microsoft Exchange Server computer that failed. If the production Microsoft Exchange-based server is a BDC, add the recovery server to the production domain as a BDC. As mentioned earlier, you need to first delete and then re-add the computer name on the PDC to create a new SID for the recovery computer. The recovery server should have a version of the Windows NT Service Pack installed that matches the configuration of the production server. Also, make sure that there is enough disk space for restoring the entire information store and directory from your backup tape. This computer should also be equipped with a tape drive that is compatible with the tape drives deployed on production servers. To expedite the restore process, maintain a copy of the Windows NT installation code and Service Pack on the hard drive of the recovery computer. For information on settings for protocol addresses, partitioning information, protocols, options, tuning, and other options, see your production Windows NT Server configuration data.

Creating a New Site But Not Joining the Existing Site

The following process will enable you to create a new site without joining the existing site.

1. Log on to Windows NT as an administrator and install Microsoft Exchange Server using the same site and organization name that was used on the server from which you are restoring the mailbox.

2. Use the Setup command to install Microsoft Exchange Server. Do not type **Setup /R**. This creates a problem that you will encounter when attempting to upgrade this recovery server to the latest Microsoft Exchange Service Pack.

3. When prompted, select **Create New Site**. Note that the server name of the recovery server matches that of the production computer.

4. Select the same service account that you used for the production server.

5. Run the Microsoft Exchange Performance Optimizer to optimize Microsoft Exchange Server for the same configuration that was used on the production server. For more information, see your production server configuration documentation.

6. After Microsoft Exchange is installed, upgrade this recovery server to the same Microsoft Exchange Service Pack as the production server.

7. Install Microsoft Exchange Client on the recovery server.

Performing the Restore

This procedure assumes that you are using an online backup tape for the restore (the backup was performed while Microsoft Exchange Server services were running). If an offline tape is used, do not choose to start the services after the restore.

After the restore, at the command prompt, type **isinteg -patch** to run the ISINTEG tool. Make sure that the directory service is started first, and then start the information store service.

▶ **To perform the restore**

1. Insert the restore tape.

2. In the **Administrative Tools** group, double-click the **Backup** icon.

3. Double-click the **Tapes** icon.

4. Double-click **Full Backup Tape**.

5. In the right pane, select the directory and information store that you want to restore.

6. Choose **Restore**.

7. In the **Restore Information** dialog box, select the following check boxes: **Erase all existing data**, **Verify After Restore**, and **Start Service After Restore**.

Note If the public information store is on a separate computer, do not select the **Erase all existing data** check box. Instead, select the following check boxes: **Private**, **Public**, **Verify After Restore**, and **Start Services After Restore**. If you erase the public store inadvertently, contact Microsoft Technical Support.

---

8. Type the name of the destination server in the **Destination Server** box.

9. Choose **OK**.

10. If the directory service and information store were backed up using separate backup jobs, do not start these services until both have been restored.

11. When the restore prompt appears, choose **OK**. This opens the **Restore Status** dialog box.

12. After the restore is completed, choose **OK**.

13. Close the Backup program.

Reviewing Mailboxes for Windows NT Account Association

To verify that your users' mailboxes have a Windows NT account associated with them, follow these steps.

1. In the Microsoft Exchange Administrator program, select a server, and then choose **Recipients**.
2. Double-click a user's name.
3. Review the **Primary Windows NT Account** box to verify that the Windows NT account matches the mailbox.

Repeat this procedure as needed for each user.

Testing a User's Logon from a Client Workstation

To test a user's logon from a Microsoft Exchange Client workstation, follow these two steps.

1. Start the Microsoft Exchange Client.
2. Verify that the user's password is accepted.

Authoritative Restore

If directory information on the restored server changes or automatically gets purged, you may be experiencing an undesired backfill state.

When previous replicated changes from the restored server are replicating back from another server, the other server may have a change record that is more up-to-date than what is reflected in the restored database. In this case, *backfilling* has occurred.

The Authoritative Restore tool (Authrest.exe) available on the Microsoft Exchange Server compact disc enables you to force a restored directory database to replicate to other servers after restoring from a backup. For assistance on using this tool, contact Microsoft Technical Support.

Normally, a restored database is assumed to be more out-of-date than the collective information held on all other directory replicas in the organization. A restored directory normally replaces its information with more recent data held by other servers. This functionality is appropriate when the reason for the restore is that a database or server was destroyed, but it is not appropriate in all cases. For example, if an administrative error deleted thousands of mailboxes or vital configuration information, the goal of restoring from backup is not to restore one server to functionality, but to move the entire system back to where it was before the undesired changes were made.

Without the Authoritative Restore tool, you would need to restore every server in the organization from a backup that predates the error, or else you would have to restore every server in the site, and then force all bridgeheads in other sites to resynchronize from scratch. If only one server was restored, or if servers were restored one at a time, the restored server would quickly overwrite its restored data with the more recent (incorrect) information held by all other servers in the site.

The Authoritative Restore tool enables you to restore one server (presumably the server with the most recent pre-mistake backup) rather than all servers. Normal replication then causes the restored information to spread to all servers throughout the organization.

The Authrest.exe file is available from the Support\Utils*<platform>* directory on the Microsoft Exchange Server compact disc.

.Pst, .Ost, and .Pab Recovery

Data recovery includes backing up and restoring three types of files:

- .Psts
- .Osts
- .Pabs

Before restoring any of these files, however, read the next section, which describes how to restore databases by using the correct version of Microsoft Exchange Server with the accompanying Service Pack.

Restoring Service Packs

When restoring databases, it is important that you run the restored databases under the same Microsoft Exchange Server version that they previously ran under. Therefore, do not start services until all code is up-to-date. For example, if you are using Microsoft Exchange Server Service Pack 2 (SP2), but have the original server compact disc and SP2 code, you should have the SP2 code loaded before running Microsoft Exchange Server with your restored databases from an SP2-level server.

After you have installed the correct Service Pack, you can restore your database files by replacing the new databases that were installed by running the Setup program. When you do so, make sure that you follow the appropriate restore procedures.

Note If you run **Setup /R**, it will not create the .Dir.edb, Pub.edb, and Priv.edb files. (Normally these files are created with the organization and site name given during setup.) **Setup /R**, however, copies the Dir.edb from the Microsoft Exchange Server compact disc exactly the way it is. You will not be able to start the directory service with the default Dir.edb.

You also must restore all database files (Dir.edb, Pub.edb, and Priv.edb). If you plan to restore only the information store and not the directory, then do not run **SETUP /R**.

Restoring from an .Ost File After Mailbox Deletion

.Ost files are "slave" replicas of Microsoft Exchange Server folders. If you delete the master, the slave is orphaned. If the original Microsoft Exchange profile was not modified, then you can start the process offline with the old .ost file, and recover the data by copying it to a .pst file. However, if the old profile was deleted or modified (for example, if you used the profile to log on to the new mailbox), the data is lost.

The reason data is lost is due to the way in which security is enforced on .ost files. You cannot perform Windows NT authentication while you're offline. Instead, you have to prove that you can log on to the server-based master before the .ost file will give you local access.

Microsoft Exchange Server does this by creating an encrypted "cookie" from your mailbox's unique entry ID, while you have successfully logged on to the server. This cookie is securely stored in your Microsoft Exchange Server profile. Your profile stores the key for the .ost file. Every time you try to access the .ost file, it checks your profile for the existence of this key.

The exception to making the .ost file non-recoverable occurs if one of the following takes place:

- You delete the master server mailbox.
- You also delete or modify the profile containing the key to the .ost file.

Using the Inbox Repair Tool to Repair .Pst and .Ost Files

The Inbox Repair Tool repairs.pst and .ost files. This tool is similar to the MMF check capability in Microsoft Mail and is installed in the Microsoft Exchange Client subdirectory.

The Inbox Repair Tool performs eight checks on the selected file. Note that during repair, you can choose to back up the existing file before making the repair. The following figure shows the Inbox Repair Tool after a scan has been performed.

Security IDs, Secret Objects, and Windows NT-Based Computer Accounts

The following figures show a Windows NT Secure Channel in a normal production environment.

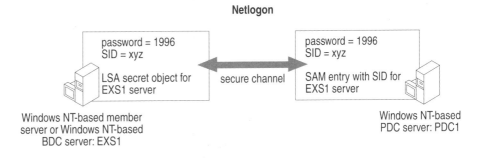

Each Windows NT Server computer has a unique SID that is used for domain authentication. Note that the Windows NT SID for EXS1 is xyz. This SID is used solely for purposes of this example, and is not the actual SID format. To connect to the domain, the Windows NT BDC (member server) must have a matching SID and local security authority (LSA) password that enables authentication to take place. The following figure illustrates a secure channel failure.

Netlogon Fails

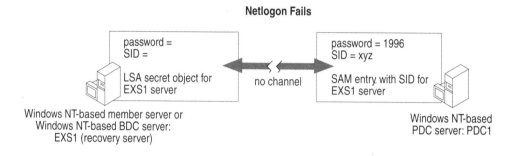

This figure demonstrates what happens if you do not first delete and then re-add the Microsoft Exchange Server computer account before installing a recovery server. If a recovery server is rebuilt by installing Windows NT from scratch, and the same computer name is used, NETLOGON will fail because the old computer account and SID remain in the domain SAM and can only be reset from within the Server Manager program by deleting and re-adding the computer account.

The following figure shows a re-established computer account.

Netlogon

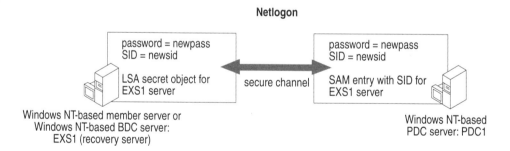

When the old computer account is deleted and then readded to the domain SAM, the SAM entry is first set to an initialize state. When the new server is added, a local LSA secret object is created along with a SID, thus synchronizing the LSA secret object (stored locally on the BDC or member server) with the SAM object for the respective computer. In addition, a password is generated that is used whenever the BDC or member server computer logs on to the domain. This process creates a secure channel between the BDC and the PDC. The secure channel password is changed automatically by NETLOGON to prevent the password from being discovered.

Note that the LSA secret object is created by Setup during the initial installation or when a server joins a domain. The SAM computer account is created by the Server Manager program.

Tips and Techniques for Dependable Disaster Recovery

There are a number of things you can do on a routine basis to ensure that your disaster recovery plan is successful. Review the topics in this section when you understand what you need to do to backup and recover files.

Create and Verify Daily Backups

This is a critical step in disaster recovery. It sounds simple, but you can only recover data if you have a valid backup. Failure to verify backups is one of the most common mistakes made. It is often assumed that backup tapes are being swapped and that data is being properly backed up. It should be a daily routine to review all backup logs and follow up on any errors or inconsistencies. Furthermore, full (normal) backups reset and remove transaction logs. This results in free disk space. Note that this is less of an issue if circular logging is enabled. If circular logging is not enabled and daily full backups are failing, transaction logs will not be purged and you can fill up the entire transaction log disk drive.

Perform Periodic File-Based Backup

To capture all configuration data, it is best to perform a full file-based backup periodically. Services should be shut down so that open files can be backed up. This will ensure that you have backed up all possible Microsoft Exchange related files. You may want to perform this backup during scheduled maintenance. Note that file-based backup is not required for backing up the information store and directory databases. Online backups are recommended for backing up the information store and directory.

Standardize Tape Backup Formats

Recovery equipment must be compatible with production tape equipment. If you deploy a new type of tape drive, make sure you that you use a compatible model for your recovery equipment. You should also test reading and restoring production tape backups on the tape drive used for recovery.

Deploy a UPS and Test it Periodically

Do not take the approach that if the Microsoft Exchange-based server does not fail during a power outage, that all other servers have not failed. Make sure you are protected by an uninterruptible power supply (UPS). Many computer rooms are supposedly UPS protected. Even though this may be the case, it is possible that not all outlets are UPS protected. If you do not have a dedicated UPS, make sure that you speak with the local electricians or operations personnel and perform a test. Also note that server class UPS system batteries can wear out every three years and require replacement.

Review the Environment When Placing Production Servers

Inspect the area when deploying servers. Make sure that the environment is receptive. For example, you should ensure that there is enough power, and if possible, dedicate power lines for your equipment. Review existing amperage and new amperage requirements. Make sure that servers are not placed under fire sprinklers. Also, make sure that your servers are in a physically secure location and that the room temperature is acceptable.

Perform a Periodic Fire Drill

A periodic fire drill is an effective way to measure your ability to recover from a disaster and to certify your disaster recovery plans. Conduct this in a test environment and attempt a complete recovery. Make sure to use data from production backups. During this process, record the time it takes to recover. This information will assist you in estimating the time it will take to recover in a real disaster recovery situation. From personal experience, up to one-third of recovery time can be spent in preparing and getting the correct tools in place to complete the job. For maximum effect, provide no notice to your staff that you are performing a drill. This will be the most valuable experience you will have in your disaster recovery planning.

Check Windows NT EventLogs Daily

Take a proactive approach and review logs regularly. This can help you identify problems before they have an impact. A number of logging tools are available in Microsoft Exchange Server and this should be leveraged.

Create a Disaster Recovery Kit

Planning ahead reduces recovery time. It is critical to build a kit that includes items such as an operating system configuration sheet, hard drive partition configuration sheet, hardware configuration sheet, Extended Industry Standard Architecture/Micro Channel Architecture (EISA/MCA) configuration disks, Microsoft Exchange Server configuration sheet, Windows NT emergency repair disk, Microsoft Exchange Performance Optimizer settings sheet, and so on.

Publish a Microsoft Exchange Server Maintenance Schedule

Perform basic preventive maintenance on a regular basis. The robustness of Microsoft Exchange Server can be compromised by failure to perform basic preventive maintenance routines when deploying servers. A Microsoft Exchange Server computer is no different than a car that requires oil changes and other maintenance. Unlike mainframes, servers are often overlooked when it comes to scheduling downtime for maintenance. It is a simple formula: Planned maintenance generally reduces unplanned downtime. It is important to set user expectation levels by publishing a maintenance schedule especially when users expect service 24 hours per day, 7 days per week. Maintenance is inevitable because the nature of the data processing business includes service pack updates, software upgrades, and hardware upgrades. Although rare, it might be necessary to take down the information store service to reduce the size of store files by using the EDBUTIL troubleshooting utility. This utility is available on the Microsoft Exchange Server compact disc.

Determine Downtime Cost

Determining the cost of downtime is useful when justifying the purchase of recovery equipment. There are different models for calculating the per-hour downtime cost, which varies for each business. These calculations include lost orders per hour, delayed financial transactions, and the cost of delayed time-sensitive market decisions. For more information on justifying disaster recovery expenditures, see the *National Computer Security Association News* (July 1996).

Consider Maintaining Off-Site Tapes and Equipment

Due to legal or security issues, certain companies choose not to send backup tapes to a third party off-site location. An alternative is to send tapes to an off-site location within the same company.

Dedicate Recovery Equipment and Build a Recovery Lab

It is important to dedicate hardware. Don't allow test equipment to become production equipment without replacement. Make sure the recovery equipment is always in working order and available at a moment's notice. Some companies purchase recovery equipment, but then install "test only" software. They become dependent on this equipment for production use. In short, keep recovery equipment in a dedicated mode. Another reason to build a lab is for recovery purposes. When you use the EDBUTIL troubleshooting utility, up to two times the disk space of the largest production server information store database is required for recovery and database defragmenting. It is more cost effective for an organization to maintain one recovery server with sufficient disk space.

Keep Accurate Records of All Configurations

This is necessary when configuring the recovery server. Records include Windows NT tuning settings, path information, protocol addresses, Microsoft Exchange Server connector configurations, and so on. These records should be part of the disaster recovery kit discussed earlier.

Take a Proactive Approach to Monitoring the Information Store

Monitor the growth of the information store and server performance. Be prepared with a plan to remedy any issues. Windows NT disk space alerts can be set up to monitor remaining disk space. Performance Monitor objects exist for the information store and should be used.

Devise an Archiving Plan

An archiving plan enables your users to move server-based messages into local store files. This reduces the size of the server-based information store. Have users store their .pst files on local drives or on a separate disk or server from the information store. Dedicate a file server for .pst archiving if required. Otherwise, data will be reduced in the information store but added to another area of the same disk or logical drive. The impact will be greater because .pst storage maintains messages in both Rich Text Format (RTF) and ASCII format. Note also that disk space limits cannot be set on .pst files. Make sure to include all sensitive data in backup strategies, including users' .pst files. Use encryption when creating .ost files and .pst files.

Consider Microsoft Exchange Server Roles

You should always avoid making your Microsoft Exchange Server computer a PDC. If this computer becomes unavailable, an alternate domain controller must be promoted to become the primary domain controller. If the Microsoft Exchange Server computer is not the PDC, you do not need to worry about promotions and demotions of domain controllers in a recovery situation.

Some companies prefer to place the Microsoft Exchange Server on a BDC in the accounts domain so that a second computer is not required for Windows NT authentication in remote offices. This can save the cost of purchasing another computer. However, make sure to account for additional RAM overhead for the Windows NT SAM, in addition to Microsoft Exchange Server memory requirements. Windows NT domain controllers require RAM equal to 2.5 times the size of the SAM.

If the Microsoft Exchange Server computer is a member server and not a PDC or BDC, additional memory overhead for the domain SAM is not required. However, for remote offices, companies can save money by using the local Microsoft Exchange Server to provide authentication (BDC) and messaging services.

Note For a proper directory service restore, access to the original SAM is required. Never install a Microsoft Exchange Server computer in a domain that does not have a BDC.

An alternative is to place the Microsoft Exchange Server computers in a large resource domain that trusts each account's domain. In this case, the Microsoft Exchange servers can be placed on BDCs without incurring significant memory overhead because the SAM for the Microsoft Exchange Server resource domain will be relatively small in size.

Locate Transaction Log Files on Separate Dedicated Physical Disks

This is the single most important aspect of Microsoft Exchange Server performance. However, there are recovery implications to maintaining transaction log files on separate dedicated physical disks. Transaction logs provide an additional mechanism for recovery.

Disable SCSI Controller Write Cache

To avoid the potential for data loss, disable the small computer system interface (SCSI) controller write cache. At a programming level, if the write-through flag is set, Windows NT will not use buffers and therefore, when a program receives a write complete signal from Windows NT, it is guaranteed that the write was completed to disk. This is critical to the Microsoft Exchange Server transaction logging process. If write cache is enabled, Windows NT thinks that a write has been made to disk and will inform the calling application of this false information. This could result in data corruption if a crash is experienced before this lazy-write operation makes it to disk.

Disable Circular Logging if Possible

Although circular logging can help conserve disk space, it disables incremental and differential backups. In addition, transaction log history is cyclical and cannot be restored. If a solid backup strategy is in place, transaction log files are purged on a regular basis, which frees disk space.

Place Limits on Information Store Attributes

Configure mailbox storage limits and maximum age of server-based messages. Also limit MTA message sizes and the size of messages that users can send. These precautions will limit the amount of data you must back up and restore in case of a disaster.

Configure MTAs

Configure the MTA frequency so that queues are cleared quickly. This prevents queued messages from accumulating in the information store. Also, design a redundant MTA path so that messages keep flowing in the event of a link outage. It is important that MTAs are able to keep up with the traffic that flows through them. This reduces messages in the information store and enables timely message delivery.

Equip Servers with Sufficient Disk Space

As mentioned earlier, offline maintenance and repair routines require up to two times the disk space of the database file being administered with the EDBUTIL utility. The following figure shows a sample configuration outlining the distribution of Microsoft Exchange Server information and local store data.

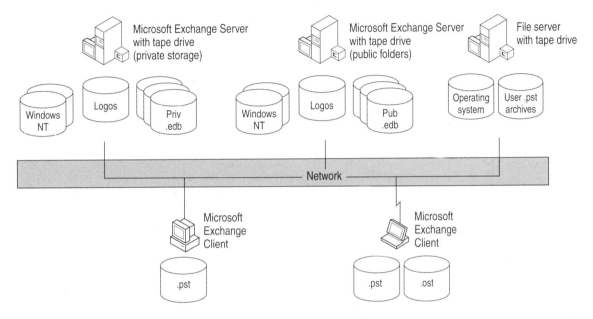

For optimal performance and recoverability, the operating system drive should be mirrored, transaction logs should be placed on a dedicated physical drive (this can also be mirrored), and the Windows NT swap file and the information store should be placed on a mirror or RAID 5 disk set.

Backup Strategies

To establish an effective backup strategy, it is important to understand the many options available to you. For example, is it better to perform full backups every night? What are the tradeoffs? Depending on business requirements, backup strategies can vary.

Time Required for Backing Up

The time required for backup depends on the backup type, as shown in the following figure.

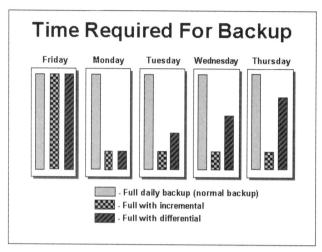

As this figure shows, performing a full backup on a daily basis requires the most time. For smaller databases, this is not an issue. However, when stored data is in the gigabyte range, it is not desirable to perform daily full backups. A full backup in combination with an incremental and or differential backup may be more appropriate in your situation.

Example A: full daily backup

This backup is performed on the following schedule: SU:F, M:F, T:F, W:F, TH:F, FR:F, S:F. The following table lists the advantages and disadvantages of this backup routine.

Advantages	Disadvantages
Always removes transaction log files	Impacts server performance the longest
Only requires one tape restore	Requires the most tape space
Simple schedule enables circular logging	Daily tape swaps usually required

Example B: Full plus one incremental backup

This backup is performed on the following schedule: SU:F, M:I, T:F, W:I, TH:F, FR:I, S:F. The following table lists the advantages and disadvantages of this backup routine.

Advantages	Disadvantages
Always removes transaction log files	Requires two tapes to restore
Multiple full backups on separate tapes	Must have knowledge of backup cycle
Incremental has much less performance impact	Circular logging must be disabled.
Tape rotations are less frequent.	
At most, two tapes required for restore	

Example C: full plus two incremental backups

This backup is performed on the following schedule: SU:F, M:I, T:I, W:F, TH:I, FR:I, S:F. The following table lists the advantages and disadvantages of this backup routine.

Advantages	Disadvantages
Always removes transaction log files	Restore requires a full backup tape, plus each incremental (in this case, up to three tapes)
Full backups are relatively frequent.	Must have knowledge of backup cycle
Little performance impact on server	Circular logging must be disabled.
Incremental requires minimal tape space.	

Example D: full plus two differential backups

This backup is performed on the following schedule: SU:F, M:D, T:D, W:F, TH:D, FR:D, S:F. The following table lists the advantages and disadvantages of this backup routine.

Advantages	Disadvantages
Full backups are frequent.	Differential backups do not remove log files.
At most, two tapes required for restore	Circular logging must be disabled.
Little performance impact	
Differential requires minimal tape space	

Summary

The strategy you choose must fit your business requirements. A general rule is to use full daily backups for small data sets. For large data sets use a combination of full, incremental, or differential backups, as outlined in examples B, C, and D. This minimizes the performance impact and the required tape space.

One common question is whether it is possible to maintain a live "hot spare" server running at all times for Microsoft Exchange Server recovery. The answer depends on how you define a hot spare.

To perform a complete server restore (which includes restoring the directory and the information store), you must configure a recovery server with the same computer name. For this reason, a secondary recovery server cannot remain online because duplicate NetBIOS names will exist. Also, two computers with the same name cannot exist within a Windows NT domain. Without restoring the Microsoft Exchange Server directory, you can recover individual mailboxes easily. However, must also reconfigure Windows NT security. This is a manual process, and therefore can be quite complex.

Examples of Online Backup Automation for IS/DS

Use the following procedure to automate online backups of the information store and directory service.

1. From the Windows NT Resource Kit compact disc, install the Winat.exe program on the local Windows NT directory of your local computer (for example, on the Winnt35 directory).

2. Create a Windows NT common group called Microsoft Exchange Server Backup.

3. Create an icon for the Winnt35\Backup.log file. This provides quick access to review the backup log.

4. Copy the Ntbackup.exe icon from the Administrative Tools group to the Microsoft Exchange Server Backup group.

5. Create an icon for Winat.exe in the Microsoft Exchange Server Backup group.

6. In Control Panel, double-click the **Services** icon.

7. Select the Schedule service and choose **Startup**. Configure for automatic startup and assign an ID that is a member of the Windows NT Backup Operators group. Make sure to enter the correct password. If the administrator ID password changes, you must change the password for the Schedule service.

8. Start the Schedule service.

9. Create the backup batch file. Name this file Back.bat and save it in the Winnt35 subdirectory.

10. Run the Winat.exe program and schedule the Back.bat file. You do not need to have a logon session on the computer in which Winat.exe is running because the Schedule service will log on to perform the operation under the defined security context. Set the batch job for interactive mode.

Sample Batch File for Online Backup

Following is a sample batch file you can use for backing up your files while the server remains online.

```
rem ** 3/7/96  Backup Written by <name>
rem ** This will back up the information store and directory service on
<server_name 1> and <server_name 2>.
ntbackup backup DS \\Server_name1 IS \\Server_name1 /v /d "Server-name1
IS-DS" /b /t Normal /l c:\winnt35\backup.log /e
ntbackup backup DS \\Server_name1 IS \\Server_name1 /a /v /d
"Server_name1 IS-DS" /b /t Normal /l c:\winnt35\backup.log /e
exit
```

Sample Batch File for Offline Backup: Example 1

You may need to experiment with the order in which you stop the services, so that you are not prompted when a service is dependent upon the one you are stopping.

```
rem ** Stop Microsoft Exchange services.
rem ** You can stop Microsoft Exchange services and restart them
automatically to backup.
rem ** Files that a particular service may hold open

REM // stop all services
echo Stopping Services...
net stop MSExchangeMSMI
net stop MSExchangePCMTA
net stop MSExchangeFB
net stop MSExchangeDX
net stop MSExchangeIMC
net stop MSExchangeMTA
net stop MSExchangeIS
net stop MSExchangeDS
net stop MSExchangeSA
ntbackup backup c:\ d:\ /a /v /d "Full File Based Backup" /b /l
c:\winnt35\backup.log /e
```

```
REM edbutil OPTIONS
net start MSExchangeSA
net start MSExchangeDS
net start MSExchangeIS
net start MSExchangeMTA
net start MSExchangeIMC
net start MSExchangeDX
net start MSExchangeFB
net start MSExchangePCMTA
net start MSExchangeMSMI
```

Sample Batch File for Offline Backup: Example 2

You can start and stop PCMTA services by enclosing the service name in quotation marks. You can determine the service names from the Microsoft Exchange Server Administrator program, the Windows NT Control Panel, or by viewing the Windows NT registry.

If you are viewing the Windows NT registry, select

HKEY_LOCAL_MACHINE, SYSTEM, CurrentControlSet, Services.

All services are listed in alphabetical order.

```
rem Batch File To Stop and Restart Microsoft Exchange Services
rem For File Based Backup
echo Stopping Services ...
net stop MSExchangeMSMI
net stop MSExchangePCMTA
net stop MSExchangeFB
net stop MSExchangeDX
net stop MSExchangeMTA
net stop MSExchangeIMC
net stop MSExchangeIS
net stop MSExchangeDS

net stop "PC MTA - HUB"
net stop MSExchangeSA
ntbackup BACKUP d:\exchsrvr\mdbdata /v /d "File Based Backup" /b /l
c:\winnt35\backup.log /e
net start MSExchangeSA
net start MSExchangeDS
net start MSExchangeIS
net start MSExchangeMTA
net start MSExchangeIMC
net start MSExchangeDX
net start MSExchangeFB
net start MSExchangePCMTA
net start MSExchangeMSMI
net start "PC MTA - HUB"
```

Windows AT Command Scheduler and the Windows NT Schedule Service

When you use the Windows AT Command Scheduler, the Windows NT Schedule service runs all jobs that have been scheduled. Because batch jobs are run in the context of the Schedule service, Windows NT security must be considered. When configuring the Schedule service, configure the account to be a member of the Windows NT Backup Operators group. This enables a full backup of the information store and directory.

The following figure shows the Windows AT Command Scheduler.

Make sure that the Back.bat jobs are set for interactive. This is required by the Ntbackup.exe program.

Information Store Recovery: a Real-World Example

Although extremely rare, the information store can become corrupted due to hardware failure or device driver failure. This section describes an actual information store recovery. The recovery procedure used was a last-resort operation. In this case, no recent backup was available and circular logging was enabled, thus preventing the playback of past transactions.

Monitoring Backup Logs and the Windows NT EventLog

When online backup of the information store fails, this may indicate that your information store is running in an inconsistent state. For this reason, it is critical to review backup logs and the Windows NT EventLog on a regular basis.

In this case, the following errors appeared in the Windows NT EventLog:

```
Event ID: 23 ; Source: EDB; Type: Error; Category: Database Page Cache;
Description: MSMicrosoft ExchangeIS ((458) Direct read found corrupted
page error -1018 ((-1:550144) (0-589866), 486912  1162627398
3480849804). Please restore the database from a previous backup.
Event ID: 8010; Source: NTBACKUP; Type: Error; Category: None;
Description:  Microsoft Exchange services returned 'c80003fa' from a
call to 'BackupRead()' additional data.
```

The Ntbackup log revealed that the online backup was failing 2.2 GB into a 3.4-GB information store backup. Until the problem could be resolved, an offline backup strategy had to be put into effect. The batch file described earlier in this chapter, in "Sample Batch File for Offline Backup: Example 2" section, was used with the Windows NT AT Command Scheduler to perform the following functions:

- Shut down Microsoft Exchange Server services.
- Perform an offline backup.
- Restart Microsoft Exchange Server.

Note that in this case, the information store appeared acceptable from a user perspective and remained functional during business hours.

Recovery Procedure

This section describes the procedure used to repair the information store.

Note This example is provided for informational purposes; you should implement the procedures described *only* with the assistance of Microsoft Technical Support. You should also note that the procedure was performed strictly in a test lab prior to being implemented in production. It is strongly recommended that you pursue the same strategy and perform all repair testing in a lab environment prior to implementing this procedure in a production environment.

The information store Prov.edb file was repaired with the EDBUTIL utility. The procedure was run on an IBM 720 server with 8-GB disk capacity and mirrored drives. The Priv.edb file was 3.4 GB.

Warning If you run the EDBUTIL utility, note that the edbutil /d /r command will delete messages. Therefore you should use this command only as a last resort.

The **EDBUTIL /D** command, however, does not delete messages and is used for offline defragmenting and reducing .edb file size. When running EDBUTIL with the /d (defragment) option, you will need available disk space up to one times the size of the .edb files you are running against (or a disk two times the size of the EDB). For example, if your Priv.edb file is 3.4 GB and there is no empty space in the file, you will need 3.4 GB of available space for the defragment operation. This does not include any swap file growth that can temporarily occur. If there is 4 GB of empty space in the Priv.edb file, you will need 3 GB of available space.

By default, the Tempdfrg.edb file will be used to rebuild the .edb file. When running EDBUTIL, you can use the **/t** option to redirect the Tempdfrg.edb file to a non-default location or to rename it. You cannot however, redirect this temporary file to a LAN-connected drive.

The following table provides estimated times for the backup actions that were performed, and a description of each action.

Action	Time	Description
Ntbackup.exe	2.5 hours	All Microsoft Exchange Server services were stopped. A file-based restore of Pub.edb and Priv.edb was performed from a recent production backup. The approach taken was to establish the production problem in a test environment. A server was built with the same organization and site name as in the production environment, but a different server name was used. The computer was also set up on a separate domain. This enabled a restore of an information store from a different computer (the production computer). Org=XYZ Site = NJ1 Server = SERVER2
Ran the following ISINTEG command: **isinteg -patch**	5 minutes	After restore, the **isinteg -patch** command was used to complete an offline information store backup. The directory service and system attendant were started prior to running this command.
Started all Microsoft Exchange Services	3 minutes	

(continued)

Action	Time	Description
Ran the DS/IS consistency adjuster	5 minutes	The information store needed to be synchronized with the directory service on the test server because only the information store files had been restored, and not the directory.
Associated Windows NT account to test mailbox	5 minutes	After the DS/IS consistency adjuster was used, a valid Windows NT ID needed to be assigned to a recovered mailbox. The Administrator program was used to associate the Windows NT account.
Tested messaging functionality	10 minutes	Sent and received several messages in the Microsoft Exchange Client to test basic messaging functionality.
Ran Windows NT Ntbackup.exe program	1.5 hours	Ran an online Ntbackup.exe job to test whether the production failure could be duplicated. At 1.5 hours, the information store backup failed 2.2 GB into the job, with an event ID 8010 error. This verified that testing was for a failing information store. The production problem was reproduced in a test environment with a copy of the production information store.
Stop Microsoft Exchange Services	3 minutes	
Ran the following EDBUTIL command **edbutil /ispriv /d /r /n**	2 hrs 30 minutes	Ran this command from the D:\Exchsrvr\Mdbdata directory to determine whether the corrupt information store could be repaired.
Ran the following ISINTEG command: **Isinteg -pri -fix -verbose -l isinteg.log**	1 hr 10 min	Ran this command against the Priv.edb and Pub.edb files.
Start Microsoft Exchange Services	~3 minutes	
Test Messaging	~10 minutes	
Ran the Ntbackup.exe program again	~2.5 hours	Performed another online backup to determine whether the problem still remained. The online backup of the information store and directory service completed successfully.

Backing Up a Key Management Server

It is recommended that you back up the KM server data files (for example, Security\Mgrent), separately from other data, and that you make sure these backup tapes more secure than your everyday backups. All keys in these files are 64-bit CAST encrypted, so this database is extremely secure. Remember that this database contains the private encryption keys for every user in your entire organization.

The problem with tape cartridges is that they are maintained offline. If someone were to steal one, that person could restore the files to his or her own server, and then try to crack the key used for the database, with no fear of detection due to online logons, and so on. For more information, see the *Microsoft Exchange Server Administrator's Guide*.

Disaster Recovery Frequently Asked Questions (FAQs)

This section provides answers to frequently asked questions regarding disaster recovery and Microsoft Exchange Server.

Q: If I have a good backup of the directory and information store and I am restoring a server to an existing site by reinstalling Microsoft Exchange Server, should I create a new site or join an existing site during the Microsoft Exchange Server installation?

A: Create a new site. Do not select **Join Existing Site**. If you attempt to join the existing site, an error will occur because other servers in the site already have knowledge of the server you are restoring. When the server is restarted after the restoration of the databases, the restored server automatically synchronizes with existing servers in the site, even though you selected **Create a New Site** during the server installation.

Q: If I want to keep a spare server online for performing single mailbox restores, should I select **Join Existing Site** or **Create a New Site** during the installation of Microsoft Exchange Server?

A: Do not select **Join Existing Site**. When maintaining a single mailbox restore server, you must configure the server with the same organization and site name as the site from which you plan to recover single mailbox data. However, it is important to repeat that you should not select **Join Existing Site** during the installation. Select **Create a New Site**. Also, use a unique computer name when installing Microsoft Windows NT. If you inadvertently join a site and then complete the single mailbox restore procedures as outlined earlier, undesired replication behavior will result after you run the DS/IS consistency adjuster because you will have two sets of mailbox data for the same users within the site after restoring a Priv.edb.

Q: I have some users that use .pst files and remain logged on at night. How can I back up their .pst files?

A: The client will automatically disconnect from the .pst file after 30 minutes of inactivity. Upon activity, the client will automatically reconnect to the .pst. Because of this feature, you can back up .pst files during periods of inactivity (usually at night) while the client is logged on to Microsoft Exchange Server.

Q: I know that I need to run **isinteg -patch** after restoring an offline information store backup to patch the globally unique identifiers (GUIDs), but what is a GUID?

A: A GUID is a 64-bit hexadecimal string. It uniquely tags an object in time and space. Within the information store, the private and public information stores have base GUIDs that they use to generate GUIDs for all other objects in the stores, including folders, messages, attachments, and so on. The patch that the ISINTEG tool performs changes the base GUIDs in the information store. The reason the patch must be run is because when you restore an information store, you are essentially rolling back time on that server. If you roll back the server and don't change the base GUID, new objects created in that information store could have GUIDs that are identical to other existing objects in the organization. This would cause problems in referencing objects, because they could no longer be uniquely identified. If you only have one server in your organization, this is not a problem, because when you restore, there are no other objects in the organization that have IDs that might be generated again for new objects.

Q: What is the tradeoff regarding location of log files? I have computers with a total of five disk drives. The first two drives are mirrored and the other three are set up in a RAID 5 stripe set? Should I not mirror the operating system and use one of those drives to dedicate for transaction log files to gain performance?

A: In Microsoft Exchange Server, the best performance is gained through dedicating a physical drive for transaction log files. This is because transaction log files are written to sequentially and on a dedicated drive, the disk read/write head will not have to contend with other processes. However, it may not be worth sacrificing operating system drive redundancy by not using a mirror set for the first two drives. In this case, it is best to maintain the Windows NT swap file and the Microsoft Exchange database files on the three-disk stripe set (RAID 5) and to maintain the transaction log files on the mirror set. With enough RAM in the system, there should be little disk head contention on the operating system drives and transaction log performance should be high.

Q: How important is transaction log file redundancy?

A: In general, transactions are committed to the databases quickly. However, on a very busy system, transactions written to log files can accumulate before being committed to the database files. If the transaction log drive crashes before transactions are written, this data will be lost.

Q: How can I shut down Microsoft Exchange Services without using Control Panel? Sometimes these services take a long time to shut down.

A: You can issue commands from the command line to shut down services or you can follow the batch file example shown below. If you want to shut down the entire system from a batch file, use the shutdown command, which is available on the Windows NT Resource Kit compact disc. The purpose of this command is to shut down services in reverse dependency order. To shut down an MTA service that includes spaces in the name, use quotation marks.

```
REM // stop all services
echo Stopping Services...
net stop MSExchangeMSMI
net stop MSExchangePCMTA
net stop MSExchangeFB
net stop MSExchangeDX
net stop MSExchangeIMC
net stop MSExchangeMTA
net stop MSExchangeIS
net stop MSExchangeDS
net stop MSExchangeSA
REM - call the shutdown command here. (Remember, this command
requires that you have the Windows NT Resource Kit compact disc.)
```

Q: My tape drive is dead, but I need to back up the databases. How can I do this?

A: If you have enough disk space, shut down services and copy the Priv.edb and Pub.edb files from the Exchsrvr\Mdbdata directory (the default installation point). Also copy the Dir.edb file from Exchsrvr\Dsadata (the default installation point). You do not need to copy the transaction log files, because when services are shut down normally, all transactions are resolved. If you need to restore from this backup method, remove the log files and Edb.chk from their respective directories, copy the .edb files back in, and follow the procedure for running **isinteg -patch**. When the services start up, a new Edb.chk file is created, along with new transaction log files. Make sure to back up any files before you purge them. If you need additional assistance with these procedures, it is recommended that you contact Microsoft Technical Support.

Q: How long does it take to defragment a database using the EDBUTIL utility?

A: The databases are defragmented automatically as a background process, so unless the file size of the databases needs to be reduced, you should not have to run offline compaction (defrag with file size reduction).

Q: Do I need a backup of the directory database to recover a server?

A: You need at least one backup of the directory service for each computer. Regardless of how old the backup is, the directory service will rebuild itself on that computer and become current from the other directory services in the site after the restore. After you have installed a new server in a site and it is replicated and current, the best thing to do is to make a backup of the directory service.

After a restore, run a DS/IS consistency check after the directory service has came back in sync. This ensures that all objects in the information store on that computer are restored back into the directory service. If you don't have a backup of the directory service for a server to restore from, your only option is to delete the server from the site and then reinstall it. This option is not advisable because you lose all your information store data.

Instead, make a backup of the directory service as soon as possible after installing a new server, and then lock the backup in a safe place. Replace the backup with more up-to-date backups on a regular basis. This way, you don't have to wait long for the directory service to come back into sync after a restore.

Q: Why do I need to back up the system following the migration of users to the server? Also, why do I need to back up the system after running an offline EDBUTIL operation?

A: If a server crashes after a migration and you have not backed up the system data, you must perform the migration again. This can be time-consuming. After you run an offline EDBUTIL operation, the database is in a new state. If your system experiences a crash, you must perform the operation again. This can also be time-consuming.

Q: When I shut down services, they keep trying to restart. Why does this happen and what can I do?

A: This problem is most likely caused by a server monitor session configured for the server in which you are trying to shut down services. By running the Administrator program **admin/t** (maintenance mode) command at least one polling interval before stopping services, you ensure that the server monitor is notified that subsequent polls of the server in maintenance mode will not result in alerts or alarms. After running this command, you can stop services and perform maintenance. When the maintenance is completed, rerun **admin /t** to re-enable monitoring. For command-line Help on Administrator program command-line switches, switch to the Exchsrvr\Bin directory and type **admin /?.**

Q: What backup strategies and solutions are being created by third parties, and what value do their solutions add?

A: To learn more about third-party solutions, visit http://www.microsoft.com/exchange/exisv/. Then perform a search on all products that use the keyword "backup". This will provide links to third-party solutions.

Q: Is it a good idea to periodically perform a directory export ?

A: Yes. It is a quick operation and will save you time if you are unable to restore your directory database in the future. You should never have to rely on this procedure, but it is an extra safety measure that will enable you to quickly add users if necessary.

Q: Where can I find more information on information store startup problems?

A: Articles in the Microsoft Knowledge Base can be provide additional information on information store startup problems, and other issues. To access the Knowledge Base, visit http://www.microsoft.com/kb. Perform a search on "Microsoft Exchange," and then enter relevant keywords.

Q: What are "lazy" commits and "non-lazy" commits, and how does Microsoft Exchange Server use them?

A: After transaction logs are flushed to disk, the transaction is durable. If your system crashes, these logs can be restored and nothing will be lost. *Non-lazy* commits retain data on the hard drive, while *lazy commits* indicate that the transaction logs have not been saved.

Q: Should I disable the SCSI controller write cache?

A: Yes. Doing so enables you to avoid the potential for data loss. At a programming level, if the write through flag is set, Windows NT will not use buffers. Therefore, when a program receives a write complete signal from Windows NT, it is guaranteed that the write was completed to disk. This is critical to the Microsoft Exchange Server transaction logging process. If write cache is enabled, Windows NT thinks that a write has made it to disk and will inform the calling application of this "false" information. This could result in data corruption if a crash is experienced before this lazy write operation makes it to disk.

Q: When is a transaction committed to the database and how does this work? Is it first cached in memory so that it is virtually available, or is it necessary to read back from log files before writing to the database files?

A: Transactions are on both log files and fast memory pages. Log disk heads are never moved back to read old data, so only sequential writes occur on log files. After transactions are written to a log file, an operation is considered complete. The transaction is immediately available in server memory before it is actually committed to the database files. Remember that an operation is not complete (that is, the Client does not receive an acknowledgment) until all transactions are written to the transaction log (on disk).

Q: How can I measure how the transaction logging process is doing?

A: Use Performance Monitor and select the **MSExchangeDB** object. Configure the following counters:

- **Log Bytes Write/sec** — The rate at which bytes are written to the log.

- **Log Checkpoint Depth** — This is proportional to the time that recovery will take after a system crash, depending on the performance of the individual system. A data page may be cached and not flushed to the .edb file for a long time. The earliest logged operations on the page can date back a significant time. To ensure that your system recovers from a crash, do not restore too many logs, and set the checkpoint depth to determine how many logs you can expect to replay during recovery.

- **Log Sessions Waiting** — The number of sessions waiting on a log commit in order to complete a transaction.

Q: What is the advantage of disabling circular logging?

A: Disabling circular logging provides for additional recoverability. This is because a history of transaction logs will be maintained for all transactions. These log files are only purged when a full or incremental online backup is performed.

They are purged because they are no longer needed after all transactions are committed to the databases and the databases are backed up. For example, suppose your last good backup occurred on Monday and on Thursday your database drive crashes. If you disabled circular logging and your transaction log files are configured on a separate physical drive from the drive that crashed, you can restore the Monday backup. In this case, you should *not* erase existing data, and you should verify that the log files created since the Monday backup have been restored back into the database. This process will restore your data to the point immediately before the crash.

Q: When I try to run the **isinteg -patch** command, it does not run and I receive the following error message: DS_E_COMMUNICATIONS_ERROR. How do I solve this problem?

A: Make sure the directory service is started before running the command.

Q: How can I back up Microsoft Exchange Server computers from a Windows NT Server backup computer that does not have Microsoft Exchange Server or the Microsoft Exchange Administrator program installed?

A: If you are copying files from an existing Microsoft Exchange Server computer, do one of the following:

- In the Winnt Root\System32 directory on the Windows NT Server backup computer, rename or delete Ntbackup.exe.

- From the Winnt Root\System32 directory on a Microsoft Exchange Server computer, copy the Ntbackup.exe, Edbbcli.dll, and Msvcrt40.dll files to the Winnt- Root\System32 directory on the Windows NT backup server.

- From the Exchsrvr\Bin directory on the Microsoft Exchange Server computer, copy Edbback.dll to the Winnt Root\System32 directory on the Windows NT Server backup computer.

Or, if you are copying files from the Microsoft Exchange Server compact disc:

- In the Winnt-Winnt-Root\System32 directory on the Windows NT Server backup computer, rename or delete the Ntbackup.exe file.

- From the Setup\platform directory on the Microsoft Exchange Server compact disc, copy the Ntbackup.exe, Edbbcli.dll, Edbback.dll, and Msvcrt40.dll files to the Winnt-Root\System32 directory on the Windows NT Server backup computer.

Q: Do I need to run the DS/IS consistency adjuster after restoring the directory and information store?

A: No. You only need to run the DS/IS consistency adjuster if you can only restore the information store. The consistency adjuster scans the information store and ensures that a directory service object exists for each information store object. If not, the directory service object is created. The consistency adjuster also scans the directory service and ensures that a corresponding information store object exists. If it does not, the directory service object is deleted. Finally, the consistency adjuster also verifies the access control list (ACL) for each object and strips any invalid entries from the list. You can also set the DS/MDB Sync diagnostic logging level to maximum and then check the application log.

Q: Should I avoid running the DS/IS consistency adjuster?

A: If you only restore the information store and must run the DS/IS consistency adjuster to re-create the directory service object for the mailboxes in the store, this sets the HOME-MDB attribute on all public folders in the hierarchy (replicas or not) to this server . In addition, it strips the public folder ACLs of any invalid entries (that is, users who do not exist in the current directory).

If you do this and then re-create a replication connector into the organization, there will be a conflict. The new server will probably win the conflict because it has newer changes to the public folder property. Accordingly, the public folder will be homed on the new server, and the new server's ACL will most likely be the ACL that is kept. This will result in lost permissions for some users.

Q: I cannot find the backup set on my tape. What might cause this?

A: Make sure that you catalog the tape before restoring any data. This process enables you to gather information on the files available on the tape, and it enables the restore process to take place. After the catalog is completed, you can start the restore process. To load a catalog of the backup sets on a tape:

- In the Tapes window, select the tape whose catalog you want loaded.

- Choose **Catalog** in one of three ways: Double-click the icon for the appropriate tape, or choose the **Catalog** button, or choose **Catalog** from the **Operations** menu.

After you search the tape, a complete list of backup sets appears in the Tapes window. Question marks are displayed in each icon to indicate that their individual catalogs have not been loaded.

Q: If you delete and re-add a computer name to the domain, and then restore the Windows NT registry from tape, is it true that the local SID from the restored Windows NT registry will not match the new SID created in the domain?

A: Yes. You should delete and re-add the name of a Microsoft Exchange Server computer in the domain only if a new server is required for recovery. The Windows NT registry should only be restored to the same physical computer because the Windows NT registry contains computer-specific data. This situation may occur if only the operating system hard disk was replaced and a Windows NT restore is performed.

Another issue to consider is that the Microsoft Exchange Server directory database maintains information about Windows NT IDs in the domain, such as ACL information. If you cannot access the SAM from the original domain and you create a new SAM by installing a new domain, and then restore the directory service, you will have a disconnect between the object security in the directory service (such as the Microsoft Exchange service account, user mailboxes, and administrator's account) and the new domain SAM. As a result, you will not be able to access any object in the Microsoft Exchange Server directory.

Q: What is the impact of configuring Microsoft Exchange Server computers as BDCs?

A: Configuring Microsoft Exchange Server computers as BDCs can provide increased recoverability and reduced costs. However, the memory requirements for these computers are also increased.

For example, suppose that a Microsoft Exchange Server computer configured as a PDC needs to be replaced. Although the Windows NT domain controller can be rebuilt and the information store can be restored, but the directory service cannot be successfully restored to a domain that does not have the original SAM.

Q: Does a full server restore to a different physical computer require the recovery server to be configured as a BDC or PDC?

A: No. The important thing is that the computer account is deleted and then re-added to the production domain so that the recovery computer can obtain a new SID that uses the same name as the original production server.

Q: How do you compact the information store databases?

A: Microsoft Exchange Server automatically compacts the information store and directory databases without interruption to messaging. Online compaction takes place in the background, marking items for deletion and defragmenting the database files.

You can also use the EDBUTIL utility to compact the information store databases. Running the **EDBUTIL /D** command reduces the size of the information store database files and defragments the database. In contrast, online compaction defragments the database files, but does not decrease their size. Note that if you use the **/D** (defragment) command-line option when running EDBUTIL, you must first stop the information store service.

Q: What is the difference between compaction, defragmentation, and information store maintenance?

A: By default, *information store maintenance* occurs between 1:00 A.M. and 6:00 A.M. The following tasks are typically completed during information store maintenance: tombstone compression, column aging, index aging, clean per user read, and message expiration. To view these settings from within the Microsoft Exchange Administrator program, select the appropriate server under **Org, Site, Configuration**. Choose **Properties** from the **File** menu, and then select the information store **Maintenance** tab.

Compaction is the the process of online defragmentation and reclaim of disk space.

Defragmentation is the offline process of reclaiming disk space and defragmenting the database files. Defragmentation is accomplished through the **EDBUTIL /D** command and will reclaim space, as well as reduce the size of the database files.

Q: At what point do log files wrap around when database circular logging is used?

A: This is usually kept to four files, but if there is a heavy load on the server, such as during a large import/migration operation or a public folder backfill, the checkpoint and window will grow greater than four log files. This does not decrease until the information store or directory service is stopped and then restarted. After the respective services are stopped and restarted, the window returns to four log files.

Q: What is the Temp.edb file and why does it get created?

A: If long-term transactions are taking place, the Temp.edb file is used to store transactions that are in progress. This file is also used for transient storage during online compaction.

Q: When should the **edbutil /d /r** command be used?

A: Only as a last resort should you use this command to repair databases. Note that this command can delete data. Before running **Edbutil /d /r**, you should always attempt a restore.

Q: What are the Res1.log and Res2.log files used for?

A: These are reserve log files that are not used unless the transaction log hard disk fills up. They are reserved for transactions that may be required to shut down the information store if the disk fills up. This way, even if the hard disk fills up, there is reserved space to record transactions from memory to disk. Note that these files are 5 MB each, regardless of the number of transactions in the log files.

Q: If an information store is in recovery after a system crash, will Microsoft Exchange Server be smart enough not to duplicate preexisting transactions in the database and only play back uncommitted transactions?

A: Yes. Log files are read and this is a very fast operation. If the transaction version number is already in the database, the transaction will not be recommitted.

Q: Will Microsoft Exchange Server automatically play back uncommitted transactions from logs when the services come up the first time following a crash?

A: Yes. If the database shut down was not clean, Microsoft Exchange Server records that and replays all transactions from the checkpoint forward at startup.

Q: If circular logging is enabled, is it true that you cannot play back logs (those that are present within the circular window)?

A: Yes. With circular logging enabled, you cannot restore from a backup and play forward. You can only restore from backup at the point the backup was taken. By default, Microsoft Exchange Server is configured with circular logging enabled.

Q: If circular logging is disabled, how can you play back transaction log files if required?

A: With circular logging disabled, you can play back logs from the last full backup. It will depend on how you are performing backups. For example, suppose that you perform a full weekly backup on Sunday and incremental backups Monday through Saturday. If you lose a hard drive or other data on Thursday, you need to restore tapes in the following order:

- Sunday: Full restore. Don't start services.
- Monday: Incremental restore. Don't start services.
- Tuesday: Incremental restore. Don't start services.
- Wednesday: Incremental restore. Don't start services.

After these restore operations are completed, start the information store service. Note that you can restore all of these backup sets in one job, and then select **Start Services** after the restore. When you do so, Ntbackup.exe will not start services until the files from all sets are restored. Ntbackup.exe will restore the data and log files from Sunday, and add the log files for Monday through Wednesday when the services restart. Finally, Ntbackup.exe will replay all log files from after the point of the full backup on Sunday until the present time (that is, Monday through Wednesday, plus any log files created after the Wednesday backup).

Incremental backups delete log files after a backup is completed. Differential backups do not delete log files; instead these files are written to tape. If you were performing differential backups, you would not need to restore the Monday through Wednesday backup because you would still have those log files on the system.

Incremental and differential backups back up all log files since the last backup, as well as the Edb.chk file. The difference between these two backup types is that differential backups do not delete log files from the system.

Q: What is the difference between running the **isinteg - fix** command and the **edbutil /d /r** command?

A: The **edbutil /d /r** command should only be run as a last resort in order to repair a database file. The **isinteg - fix** command repairs high-level objects, while **edbutil /d /r** repairs low-level database corruption. The **isinteg - fix** command repairs any "scheme" and other high level data/structure problems. If you need to run both commands, run **edbutil /d /r** first and then run **isinteg - fix**. Note that you should only run both commands if you don't have a backup to restore from and log files to play forward.

Restoring data from a backup and then playing logs forward is the recommended way to restore a corrupted database due to hardware failure. These procedures are recommended because they enable you to recover all your data. If you do not have a backup to restore and run the **edbutil /d/r** and **isinteg - fix** commands instead, you will lose all your data.

Q: Can Microsoft Exchange Server perform information store compression on the fly? Should administrators perform manual compression on a periodic basis?

A: Microsoft Exchange Server can perform online *compaction*, which is different than compression.

Microsoft Exchange Server reuses the space before growing the file. So, database defragmentation takes place in the background on a running server. The only time you should have to shut down a server for offline compaction is if you want to physically recover the free space on the disk. To reduce .edb file size, stop Microsoft Exchange services and then run the **edbutil /d** command.

Q: What is the purpose of log files?

A: On a Microsoft Exchange Server computer, the public information store, private information store, and the directory service each have log files. These files are the transaction logs for all transactions that occur on the database. In the event of a system crash, hard drive failure, power failure, or another disaster, these files can be used for soft and hard recovery and for restore after backup. The Priv.edb file on a running server is always inconsistent, due to the database cache that is in RAM on the server. The consistent state of a server is made up of the data in the .edb file and the data in the memory cache on the server. If a server computer crashes and you don't replay the logs, this will result in a corrupt database.

The log files permit automatic playback of transactions that have occurred on the database but are not yet committed to the .edb file. There is a check point (Edb.chk) that contains the current transaction point in the log files that have been committed to disk.

Log files continue to consume disk space until you do one of the following:

▪ Back up the server (by performing a full backup or an incremental backup). This writes all logs to the tape up to the check point and then deletes the logs written to tape from the hard drive. If you have to restore the database, the backup copies the database file from the tape, replays the logs on the tape, and then replays all the logs on the disk.

▪ Run with circular logging enabled.

If you browse the .edb file directories, note that you will also see *.pat files. These files are created when a backup is performed and contain all the changes (patches) since the backup started. You can write the patch file when performing a backup and be completely current. The following table lists files that you would see in the Exchsrvr\Mdbdata directory.

File	Description
Priv.edb	Private database file.
Pub.edb	Public database file.
Edb.log	Current latest log file being written to.
Edbxxxxx.log	Previous log files no longer opened or being used; new .log file every 5 MB.

(continued)

File	Description
Res1.log	Two log files are reserved in case the database or log file drive fills up the server.
Res2.log	
Priv.pat	Backup patch file for Priv.edb.
Pub.pat	Backup patch file for Pub.edb.
Edb.chk	Checkpoint file.

Monitoring Disk Space

An administrator can observe disk space usage on the drive containing the information store by using the Windows NT Performance Monitor. The LogicalDisk object, along with the "% Free Space" and "Free Megabytes" counters, are used to monitor and trigger alerts when disk space is low.

Recovering Space Used by Log Files

Increasing log files can cause the information store or directory to run out of operating space. To prevent this, do one of the following:

- Write the log files to a different drive.

- Change the location where the information store or directory store transaction logs are written. To do so, select the server object. From the **File** menu, choose **Properties**, and then select the **Database Paths** tab. Change the path names for the information store and directory transaction logs, and then choose **OK**.

- Back up the Microsoft Exchange Server computer.

- Use Ntbackup.exe to perform a normal (full) or incremental online backup of the server. This utility automatically deletes transaction logs that are no longer needed (they have been committed to disk). If you do not run Ntbackup.exe, the log files will continue to grow.

- Circular logging writes log files, but after the checkpoint has been advanced, the inactive portion of the transaction logs are discarded. Typically, this represents the majority of the potential log data. The total size of the active transactions are less than the total amount of RAM on a given computer. Therefore, with circular logging enabled, the system has complete recoverability with respect to hard and soft crashes. The element that is sacrificed is the protection against media failure. These methods are not supported on servers where circular logging is enabled, because the transaction logs are used for incremental and differential backups.

- If possible, delete any sample applications to free additional disk space.

Q: Why do I need to run the isinteg -patch command after running an offline information store restore and before starting the information store service?

A: To guarantee that GUIDs are unique. If a copy of the information store (Pub.edb and Priv.edb) is restored from an offline backup and **isinteg -patch** has not been run, when the service is restarted, it will fail, and a -1011 error will be generated. The -1011 error will produce an entry in the Windows NT Event Viewer Application Log with source ID 2048. The error message will read as follows:

The information store was restored from an offline backup. Run **isinteg -patch** before restarting the information store.

This error occurs because the GUIDs used by the information store that was restored are old and matching GUID may already exist. The GUID for this restored information store needs to be replaced to ensure that it is unique.

A command prompt error ("DS_E_COMMUNICATIONS ERROR") will also appear.

Procedure for patching the information store

To replace the GUIDs used by the restored information store, you need to run **isinteg -patch.** This command enables the ISINTEG utility to run in patch mode against the entire information store (Pub.edb and Priv.edb) and generate new GUIDs. Replication information will also be patched to prevent incorrect backfilling.

To run the **isinteg -patch** command, do the following:

- Ensure that the directory and system attendant services are running. If these services are not running, ISINTEG will fail (with a DS_COMMUNICATIONS_ERROR message).

- At the command prompt, switch to the Exchsrvr\Bin directory, and then type **isinteg -patch**.

The GUIDs will be replaced and the ISINTEG will report that the information store has been updated. At this point, you need to restart the information store service.

Q: When restoring a server in a site, if I do not have a backup of the directory (Dir.edb) for the server, can I backfill the directory from a replica on another server in the site?

A: No. It is critical that you have a backup of the directory for each Microsoft Exchange Server computer because the directory is unique for each computer. Even if you only have the original directory backup, you can restore this backup and then backfill changes from another server in the site.

Q: What is the Microsoft Exchange Server setup /r command used for?

A: The **setup /r** command enables recovery of an existing Microsoft Exchange Server computer to new hardware. Restoration of a valid database backup is also required. Run the **setup /r** command when you want to move a server installation to a different computer or if you are restoring data to a new computer.

The figure below shows the message that appears when you run the **setup /r** command.

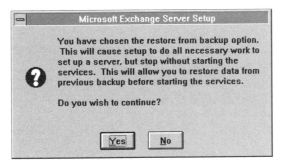

Q: Is a differential backup required only when both the transaction drive and the .edb drive need to be recovered?

A: Yes. If circular logging is disabled and the transaction logs are intact, you can restore the last full backup. When the service is started, logs from the point of the full backup will be played through the current Edb.log file to bring the database up-to-date. In this case, do *not* select **Erase all existing data** during the restore, or the transaction logs will be erased and you will need to restore the differential tape.

Q: Why can't I start services between restoring a full tape and a differential or incremental tape, or between sequential tapes being restored?

A: This is because at the end of a restore, Microsoft Exchange Server plays back all logs in sequential order. After this is done, the database is set to a new state. For example, if the services are started between a Monday incremental tape restore and a Tuesday incremental tape restore, a new state will be set. When you attempt to perform the Tuesday incremental restore, the restore will not be possible because the state of the database is expected to be exactly what it was at the point of the Tuesday backup. This behavior prevents overwriting new operations that have occurred on the database after services have been started.

Command-Line Switches for Ntbackup.exe

When you want to back up your files manually, you can use command-line switches with Ntbackup.exe.

Note In a batch file, limit the command line to 256 characters. Exceeding this limit may result in files not being backed up and may stop the process without warning.

The syntax for this command is as follows:

Ntbackup operation path [/**a**][/**v**][/**r**][/**d**"*text*"][/**b**][/**hc**:{**on** | **off**}] [/**t**{option}][/**l**"*file name*"][/**e**][/**tape**:{n}]

Switch	Description
Operation path	If you are backing up a drive, specifies one or more paths of the directories to be backed up. If you are backing up Microsoft Exchange Server components, specifies the component and the server as {directory service server /information store server}. Server is the name of the server you are backing up, preceded by two backslashes. Directory service indicates that you are backing up the directory, and information store indicates that you are backing up the information store.
/a	Causes backup sets to be added after the last backup set on the tape. When **/a** is not specified, the program reuses the tape and replaces previous data. When more than one drive is specified but **/a** is not, the program overwrites the contents of the tape with the information from the first drive selected and then appends the backup sets for the remaining drives.
/v	Verifies the operation.
/v /r	Restricts access.
/d "text"	Specifies a description of the backup contents.
/b	Specifies that the local registry be backed up.
/hc:on or **/hc:off**	Specifies that hardware compression is on or off.
/t {*option*}	Specifies the backup type. Option can be one of the following: normal, copy, incremental, differential, or daily.
Normal	All selected files or Microsoft Exchange Server components are backed up and marked as such on the disk.
Copy	All selected files or Microsoft Exchange Server components are backed up, but they are not marked as such on the disk.
Incremental	Among the selected files or Microsoft Exchange Server components, only those that have been modified are backed up and marked as such on the disk.

(continued)

Switch	Description
Differential	The selected files or Microsoft Exchange Server components that have been modified are backed up, but are not marked as such on the disk.
Daily	Among the selected files, only those that have been modified the same day are backed up, but they are not marked as such on the disk. This can be useful if you want to take work home and need a quick way to select the files that you worked on that day. This option is not available when backing up Microsoft Exchange Server components.
/l "file name"	Specifies the file name for the backup log.
/e	Specifies that the backup log include exceptions only.
/tape:{*n*}	Specifies the tape drive to which the files should be backed up. N is a number from zero to nine that corresponds to the tape drive number listed in the registry.

EDBUTIL

EDBUTIL is a utility that can be used to maintain Microsoft Exchange Server databases. The modes of operation for this tool are outlined below.

Operation	Syntax
Defragmentation	**Edbutil /d** *<database name>* **[options]**
Recovery	**Edbutil /r [options]**
Consistency	**Edbutil /c** *<database name>* **[options]**
Backup	**Edbutil /b** *<backup path>* **[options]**
Upgrade	**Edbutil /u** *<database name>* **/d***<previous .dll>* **[options]**
File dump	**Edbutil /m[mode-modifier]** *<file name>*

Defragmentation and Compaction

You can use the EDBUTIL utility to defragment and compact the data on your hard drive.

To perform an offline compaction of a database, use the following syntax: **edbutil /d** *<database name>* **[options]**

Option	Description
<Database name>	File name of database to compact, or one of the following: **/ispriv, /ispub, or /ds**
Options	Zero or more of the following switches, separated by a space: /l*<path>* - location of log files (default is the current directory).

(continued)

Option	Description
/s<path>	Location of system files.
/r	Repairs database while defragmenting.
/b<db>	Creates backup copy under the specified name.
/t<db>	Sets the temporary database name with a default name of Tempdfrg.edb.
/p	Preserves temporary database
/n	Instructs the program to dump defragmentation information to the Dfrginfo.txt file.
/o	Suppresses the logo.

The **/ispriv**, **/ispub**, and **/ds** switches use the registry to automatically set the database name, log file path, and system file path for the appropriate Microsoft Exchange Server store (public or private). Before defragmentation begins, soft recovery is always performed to ensure that the database is in a consistent state. If you disable instating by using the **/p** switch, the original database is preserved uncompacted, and the temporary database will contain the defragmented version of the database.

Recovery

Recovery is a utility that brings all databases to a consistent state. This utility is used in conjunction with EDBUTIL. The correct syntax is **edbutil /r [options]**.

Switch Option	Description
/is or /ds	The /is and /ds switches use the registry to automatically set the log file path and file path for recovery of the appropriate Microsoft Exchange stores (public or private).
/l<path>	Location of log files.
/s<path>	Location of system files.
/o	Suppresses the logo.

Consistency

To verify the consistency of a database, you can use the EDBUTIL utility with specific switches. The correct syntax is **edbutil /c <database name> [options]**. The options are zero or more of the switches as detailed in the table below. The switches must be separated by a space.

Switch Option	Description
<Database name>	File name of database to verify, or **/ispriv**, **/ispub**, or **/ds**.
/a	Checks all nodes, including deleted nodes.
/k	Generates key usage statistics.
/p	Generates page usage statistics.
/t<name>	Performs a check on the specified table only (default: checks all tables in the database).
/o	Suppresses the logo.

The consistency checker performs no recovery and always assumes that the database is in a consistent state. If the database is not in a consistent state, an error message is returned. The **/ispriv**, **/ispub**, and **/ds** switches use the registry to automatically set the database name for the appropriate Microsoft Exchange Server store (public or private).

Upgrade

You can upgrade a database that was created using a previous release of Microsoft Exchange Server to the current version. The correct syntax for performing this function is **edbutil /u** *<database name>* **/d<previous .dll> [options]**.

Note This utility should only be used to upgrade a database after an internal database format change has occurred.

The following table is a list of the parameters and options to use with EDBUTIL when upgrading a database. For options, you can use zero or more of the switches, separated by a space.

Parameters and Options	Description
<Database name>	File name of the database to upgrade.
/d<previous .dll>	File name of the .dll file that came with the release of Microsoft Exchange Server from which you are upgrading.
/b<db>	Makes a backup copy under the specified name.
/t<db>	Sets the temporary database name with a default name of Tempupgd.edb.
/p	Preserves the temporary database indicating not to instate.
/n	Dumps the upgrade information to a file called Upgdinfo.txt.
/o	Suppresses the logo.

Before you upgrade the database, the database should be in a consistent state. If the database is not in a consistent state, an error message will be returned. If you disable instating by using the **/p** switch, the original database is preserved unchanged, and the temporary database will contain the upgraded version of the database.

File Dump

The File Dump utility generates formatted output of various database file types. The correct syntax for using this utility is **edbutil /m[mode-modifier]** *<file name>*.

Parameters and Switch Options	Description
[mode-modifier]	An optional letter designating the type of file dump to perform. Valid values are: h (dump database header) and k (dump checkpoint file).
<file name>	The name of file to dump, where the type of the specified file should match the dump type being requested.

ISINTEG

The ISINTEG utility is a Microsoft Exchange Server information store integrity checker. The correct syntax for using this utility is:
isinteg -pri|-pub [-fix] [-verbose] [-l log file name] [-test test name,...]

The following table describes the switch options, parameters and their description.

Parameters and Options	Description
-pri	Private information store
-pub	Public information store
-fix	Check and correct, with check only as the default.
-verbose	Report verbosely.
-l file name	The default file name is \isinteg.pri|pub.
-test test name	The default is all tests.
Folder message	aclitem
Mailbox message	delfld acllist rcvfld timedev rowcounts
Attach message	morefld oofhist peruser
Attach global	searchq dlvrto namedprop

(continued)

Parameters and Options	Description
Ref count tests	msgref attachref acllistref aclitemref fldrcv fldsub
Special tests	deleteextracolumns (not included in all)
isinteg -patch	Repair information store after an offline restore.
-patch ()	**isinteg -pri|-pub -dump [-l logfilename] (verbose dump of store data)**

Server Configuration Sheets

The following tables illustrate examples of server configuration sheets that you can use when setting up your hardware and software specifications.

Hardware Configuration

You can use the following hardware table when specifying hardware requirements for your organization.

Hardware Item	Description
Computer Model	
Display Model	
S/N	
BackPlane	
CPU	
Hard Disk(s)	
Floppy Disk	
RAM	
NIC	
SCSI Card	
CD-ROM	
Tape Backup	

Windows NT Installation Configuration

You can use the following Windows NT installation table when specifying requirements for your organization.

Item	Description
Windows NT Server Version	
Windows NT Server Role	
Domain Name	
Computer Name	
Install Director	
Swap File	
Protocols	
Disk Configuration	
Licensing	
Printer	
Special Groups	

Item	Address
This Machine IP -	
Subnet Mask	
Default Gateway	

Microsoft Exchange Server Installation

You can use the following table when specifying Microsoft Exchange Server requirements for your organization.

Item	Description
Org Name	
Site Name	
Computer Name	
Service Account	
Service Account Password	
Connectors	

Microsoft Exchange Performance Optimizer

Running the Microsoft Exchange Performance Optimizer is important during recovery to ensure that the recovery server is tuned properly. Hardware being equal, similar performance can be experienced following a full restore where Microsoft Exchange Server is reinstalled to a recovery server. Note that the Performance Optimizer log stored in the Winnt35\System32 directory does not expose the specific settings that were chosen during optimization.

Server Name: _____

Estimated Number of Users	X	Type of Server	X	Number in Organization	X	Limit Memory Usage
1 to 25		Private information store		Less than 100		____MB
26 to 50		Public information store		100 to 999		
51 to 100		Connector/directory import		1,000 to 9,999		
101 to 250		Multiserver		10,000 to 99,999		
251 to 500				100,000 or more		
More than 500						

Component Locations

The following table lists the name s of Microsoft Exchange Server components and their locations.

Component	Location
Private information store	Exchsrvr\Mdbdata
Public information store	Exchsrvr\Mdbdata
Information storelLogs	Exchsrvr\Mdbdata
Directory service	Exchsrvr\Dsadata
Directory service logs	Exchsrvr\Dsadata
Message transfer agent	Exchsrvr\Mtadata
Internet Mail Service	Exchsrvr\Imcdata

Additional Information Sources

Following are sources of additional information on planning or maintaining a disaster recovery plan in your organization.

- For updates to the information in this chapter, visit: http://www.microsoft.com/exchange/evalgd.htm

- To view Microsoft Exchange Deployment Conference papers online, visit: http://www.microsoft.com/exchange/presentations.htm

- Microsoft TechNet: (800) 344-2121; technet@microsoft.com

- Microsoft Knowledge Base: http://www.microsoft.com/kb/

- Microsoft Knowledge Base Article Q154792: "Exchange and Schedule+ White Papers and Their Locations."

- Microsoft Knowledge Base Article Q155269:"Microsoft Exchange Administrators' FAQ."

- *Microsoft Exchange Server Administrator's Guide* (Chapter 15)

- *Microsoft Exchange Server Concepts and Planning Guide*

- Microsoft Exchange home page: www.microsoft.com/Exchange/

- Public Listserver (not maintained by Microsoft):
  E-mail msexchange-request@insite.co.uk with the word SUBSCRIBE in the message body.
  Note that this list will generate several dozen messages per day.

- Public Listserver (not maintained by Microsoft):
  E-mail msexchange-digest-request@insite.co.uk with the word SUBSCRIBE in the message body.
  You will receive one long message each day with postings from that day.

- MSNEWS network news transfer protocol (NNTP) server: msnews.microsoft.com

- Microsoft Press® Books (MSPRESS): United States (800) MSPRESS; Canada (800) 667-1115

- Microsoft Consulting Services (MCS): U.S. (800) 426-9400; Canada (800) 563-9048

- Microsoft Solution Provider Program: (800) SOLPROV

- National Computer Security Association: http://www.ncsa.com

C H A P T E R   5

Application Development

This chapter describes how you can develop custom Microsoft Exchange Server solutions to make business communications easier. The following topics are discussed:

- The scope of applications that can be developed.

- The role each component plays in providing these solutions.

- The capabilities of each component, demonstrated through customer scenarios.

Applications range from those that can be created by novice users modifying existing sample applications, to complex groupware applications developed with high-end development tools such as the Microsoft Visual Basic® programming system and the Visual C++® development system.

The Microsoft Exchange Server Infrastructure

Microsoft Exchange Server provides application development capabilities within an easy-to-administer infrastructure for messaging and replicated databases. This infrastructure includes the following components:

- **Microsoft Exchange Server** — Includes client and server software, including the directory service, information store, Message Transfer Agent (MTA), and System Attendant.

- **Microsoft Exchange Client** — Includes clients for the MS-DOS®, Windows® 3.1, Windows NT Workstation, and Windows 95 operating systems. These clients enable users to find the important information, structure it in a meaningful way, and build common information-sharing solutions without relying on the information services (IS) department.

- **Microsoft Outlook™ Client** — Includes clients for the Windows NT Workstation and Windows 95 operating systems. The Outlook client is a desktop management system that integrates messaging, scheduling, contact, task and file management into one environment.

- **Microsoft Schedule+** — Makes it easy to organize meetings, resources, tasks, and contact information, and provides a programmatic interface for integrating these capabilities into custom solutions.

- **Microsoft Exchange Forms Designer** — A Microsoft Windows-based forms-design capability that enables users to develop forms-based applications for Windows without programming, and generates Visual Basic source code for additional customization.

- **Microsoft Exchange Server sample applications** — Provide examples and source code for three categories of applications:

  - Applications designed with the tools available in Microsoft Exchange Server.

  - Customized Visual Basic–based applications integrated with Microsoft Exchange Server.

  - Server applications that run as a service of Windows NT Server and can be integrated with Microsoft Exchange Server.

- **The MAPI subsystem** — Microsoft Exchange Server is built on an open, widely used set of messaging application programming interfaces known as MAPI. These programming interfaces enable developers to use tools such as OLE Messaging (an OLE Automation interface to MAPI) OLE Scheduling (an OLE Automation interface to Schedule+), and MAPI itself.

Understanding the MAPI Subsystem

The following diagram shows the MAPI subsystem infrastructure on which Microsoft Exchange Server is built.

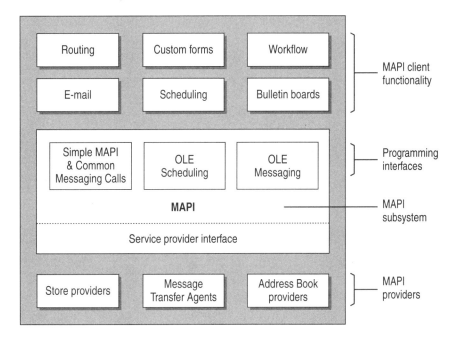

Messaging client applications either communicate with service providers through the MAPI subsystem, or the MAPI subsystem initiates contact and the services communicate directly. Through broad publication of messaging APIs, and their robust messaging and workgroup functionality, MAPI has become a widely used standard throughout the industry for messaging and groupware clients and providers.

As the previous diagram shows, MAPI-compliant clients span a variety of messaging- and workgroup-based applications and support either 16-bit applications running on Windows 3.x, or 16-bit or 32-bit MAPI applications running on Windows NT Server or Windows 95. Each of these types of applications can access the service provider functionality needed without requiring a specific interface for each provider. This is analogous to applications that use the Microsoft Windows printing subsystem not requiring drivers for every available printer.

Messaging applications that require messaging services can access them through any of five MAPI subsystem interfaces:

- Simple MAPI (sMAPI)
- Common Messaging Calls (CMC)
- OLE Messaging/Active Messaging
- OLE Scheduling
- MAPI itself

Client requests for messaging services are processed by the MAPI subsystem—either as function interface calls (for sMAPI or CMC) or as manipulations of MAPI objects (for OLE Messaging or MAPI itself)—and are passed on to the appropriate MAPI-compliant service provider. The MAPI service providers then perform the requested actions for the client and pass the action back through the MAPI subsystem to the MAPI client.

Each MAPI subsystem interface provides specific functionality as follows:

- **sMAPI** — Contains 12 Windows-based function calls that enable messaging-aware applications to perform basic messaging tasks such as sending e-mail and resolving conflicts in e-mail names. It provides the programming interface primarily used by Microsoft Mail Server.

- **CMC** — Provides functionality similar to that available in sMAPI but also supports cross-platform configurations.

- **OLE Messaging** — An OLE Automation server that presents a large subset of MAPI functionality to the developer. OLE messaging empowers developers using Visual Basic or Visual Basic for Applications to tap into the messaging and workgroup functionality inherent in MAPI. It also permits users to maximize their software investment, by integrating applications created with Visual Basic for Applications and desktop software into custom Microsoft Exchange Server solutions.

- **OLE Scheduling** — An OLE Automation server that provides developers who use Visual Basic or Visual Basic for Applications with an interface to access the information stored in Microsoft Schedule+ 7.0.

- **MAPI** — A Component Object Model (COM) interface that enables MAPI objects such as messages, forms, and folders to be manipulated. It was designed to be used by complex messaging and groupware applications. For this reason, MAPI is used by developers who want the full range of MAPI functionality in their applications and the higher performance of writing directly to an API.

Not shown in the preceding diagram, but frequently employed, are third-party programming interfaces that can be built upon MAPI. Because MAPI is an open and well-defined interface, a proprietary third-party API can be implemented on top of MAPI without having to revise the MAPI subsystem itself. You can also implement your own MAPI solutions to meet your particular needs without incurring the development costs that would otherwise accrue on other messaging infrastructures.

Integrating Schedule+ Applications

In addition to the MAPI interfaces, Schedule+, a key component available with Microsoft Exchange Client, includes an OLE Automation interface known as OLE Scheduling. Developers using Visual Basic and Visual Basic for Applications can readily integrate Schedule+ into their applications.

For example, you can use the telephony application programming interface (TAPI) and Schedule+ to create an application that sends Schedule+ meeting reminders, including a text message, to a user's pager. Or, using Microsoft Project, tasks can be scheduled in both Microsoft Project and Schedule+.

Tight integration between Microsoft Office for Windows 95 and Schedule+ enables you to quickly build applications that integrate that suite of applications, by using Visual Basic for Applications through the OLE Scheduling interface. For example, you can create an application that enables new contact information entered into Schedule+ by a company's sales force to be copied to Microsoft Excel for reporting and analysis, and reports to be generated in Microsoft Word based on information in Schedule+.

Building a Range of Solutions on a Single Platform

Most organizations need a wide range of business applications to improve processes and respond to competitive opportunities. In many organizations, this results in a heterogeneous collection of operating systems, e-mail systems, security platforms, and user directories, and the corresponding overhead of supporting those systems, training users on a variety of interfaces, and hiring a development staff versed in a wide array of technologies.

By providing an extensible messaging platform upon which users can access and build messaging and groupware, Microsoft Exchange Server eliminates the need for duplicating security systems, user directories, client interfaces, systems management interfaces, and development technologies that often accompany process-automation solutions. Microsoft Exchange Server doesn't require its own security system; it simply uses that of the operating system.

Because Microsoft Exchange Server is built on MAPI, custom-application developers and third-party software developers can write to a powerful, widely accepted programming interface to provide customers with a wide selection of groupware applications. By bringing these components under the control of a single messaging-based platform, organizations can focus their resources on creating customized applications, rather than on managing the complexities of multiple and often incompatible systems for each type of messaging or workgroup application.

Factors to Consider When Automating Business Processes

Most organizations recognize the importance of automating business processes. But most organizations must also consider a number of fundamental questions before they can determine what processes should be automated and how to automate them. These considerations include:

- What kind of applications do my users need?
- What are the associated development costs?
- What if I want to add custom functionality to those applications?

Building Common Groupware Applications

Building applications on a messaging server goes well beyond simply sending rich-text notes with attachments. Microsoft Exchange Server includes built-in groupware for routing, discussion, reference, and tracking applications. Microsoft Exchange Server also supports highly customized groupware applications and can even be integrated into customized desktop or Microsoft BackOffice server applications. The following sections describe typical groupware applications supported natively by Microsoft Exchange Server.

Routing Applications

Microsoft Exchange Server enables end users to easily create person-to-person routing forms. For example, a sales manager can design a form to gather weekly sales data from salespeople. Any salesperson, whether connected to the network or mobile, can fill out the pre-addressed form and send it back to the sales manager.

Discussion Applications

Microsoft Exchange Server also supports *discussion*, or *bulletin board* applications. These applications enable users to discuss topics with their co-workers through public folders, rather than carrying out conversations over e-mail and wading through their Inbox to find relevant e-mail threads.

Reference Applications

Most organizations need a central repository where users can find information. Microsoft Exchange Server *replicated public folders* provide a useful infrastructure for this type of application. Employee handbooks, product information, monthly reports, and sales data are all examples of useful information that can be published in public folders.

You can also make Internet newsgroups easily accessible to public folder users by developing applications for the Microsoft Exchange Internet Mail Service and the Internet News Service.

Tracking Applications

In most organizations, salespeople need to access information sources before making an account call. They may need to call other salespeople to determine who last contacted the customer, or review sales orders to find out whether the customer has outstanding orders. Many organizations provide this functionality through third-party products. Microsoft Exchange Server tracking applications eliminate this complexity and bring tracking functionality under the same user interface as other groupware applications.

For example, by creating a customer-tracking public folder, a salesperson can find information on the last contact with the customer, new customer contacts, and the company profile in a single location.

Microsoft Exchange Client enables salespeople to customize the way they display data, to view the information in the same interface as other Microsoft Exchange Server applications, and to use custom forms designed with Microsoft Exchange Forms Designer to organize and report the information. The following figure illustrates a customized view that enables users to view account data by company.

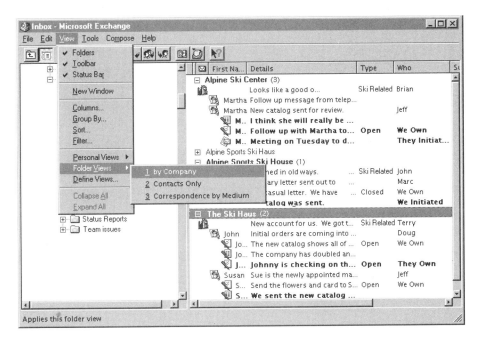

Cutting Development Costs

Competitive pressures dictate that organizations must find ways to reduce the time it takes to complete processes and access information. As a result, organizations are constantly building custom workgroup solutions. Organization-wide workgroup solutions are typically built by professional software developers who are part of the IS department. At the departmental level, solutions are often developed by technical "power users" who have learned how to write programs.

Both of these development resources are expensive, and so are the solutions they provide. Because custom solutions are in high demand, IS departments are overwhelmed with requests for new software systems and enhancements to existing solutions. As a result, solutions usually take a long time to be delivered and are difficult to modify when business conditions change, as they inevitably do.

Creating Simple Applications Without Programming

Programming creates a major obstacle to developing many custom solutions. Although programming is required for more complex applications, it hinders users who are willing to build simpler systems but lack programming skills.

If users could build their own solutions without writing programs, IS departments would have more time to focus their resources on building organization-wide systems. Users at the departmental and group levels wouldn't have to wait as long to get what they need. At the same time, programmers would benefit from a development environment that can support advanced and highly specialized solutions designed to solve more demanding problems.

Developing Scalable Applications

Microsoft Exchange Server includes a scalable set of tools that enables almost anyone, even users who have never programmed, to develop custom groupware applications. It also enables professional programmers to build advanced business software systems. The following sections describe key Microsoft Exchange Server features that enable end users and programmers to create custom solutions.

Rapid Application Development Without Programming

The Microsoft Exchange Server application design environment enables users to build complete groupware applications, such as customer-tracking systems or electronic discussion forums, without programming. Assuming they have the appropriate permissions, users can copy an existing application (including forms, views, permissions, and rules) and modify it as needed with the functionality available in Microsoft Exchange Client. They can easily modify existing forms or create new ones with Microsoft Exchange Forms Designer, which requires no programming knowledge.

Central Application Management

After users complete an application, they will usually hand it off to an administrator for further testing or distribution to others within the organization. The Microsoft Exchange Server replication engine manages the distribution of the application or any new forms that may have been revised or created for existing applications. You can also replicate these applications from one Microsoft Exchange Server site to another over the Internet by using the Microsoft Exchange Internet Mail Service.

Both of these capabilities translate into reduced cycles for creating, modifying, and distributing groupware applications. This means that end users can build applications that are valuable to them without having to wait for a response from IS. The IS department can further customize these applications, because forms created or modified with Microsoft Exchange Forms Designer are extensible with the Visual Basic programming system. With the Microsoft Exchange Server replication engine, revisions and new applications can be deployed inexpensively as well.

In summary, the rapid application design and delivery process made possible by Microsoft Exchange Server enables those who have the best understanding of the functionality needed for specific applications to respond quickly to their organization's requirements. As a result, an organization can dramatically reduce the costs of adapting and rolling out those applications.

Application Extensibility

As mentioned earlier, Microsoft Exchange Forms Designer permits end users to create forms for public folder and routing applications, without programming. It also enables software developers to customize an application further by generating Visual Basic source code for the form developed. For example, Forms Designer can generate the source code required to send a form through e-mail or to post a form in a folder. To customize forms even further, advanced programmers can use Visual Basic, Professional Edition.

Other workgroup application design tools either require a high degree of programming skill or become outdated whenever an application requires additional functionality. Microsoft Exchange Server bridges the gap between end-user application design and more powerful programming languages.

Sample Applications

The following sample applications included with Microsoft Exchange Server demonstrate the range of customizability that can be supported. The source code for each of these applications is available on the Microsoft Exchange Server 5.0 compact disc.

Chess Sample Application

The Chess sample application shown in the figure below is a custom application written in Visual Basic. This application displays the moves that have been played in a chess game between two Microsoft Exchange Server users.

The right side of the chess board displays the moves made so far. If you click one of the earlier moves, the chess pieces rearrange themselves to the positions they occupied at that point in the game.

This application demonstrates how *any* application can be created to view information in a Microsoft Exchange Server public folder or browse information in the public folder. And that application can act as the interface through which data is moved in and out of Microsoft Exchange Server, independent of the Microsoft Exchange Client.

Survey Sample Application

The Survey sample application is another example of the level of customization that can be incorporated into Microsoft Exchange Server groupware applications. It is a reusable survey design tool that enables end users to create surveys, either from scratch or by using another survey as a starting point. The sample application was developed with Visual Basic.

The following figure shows a survey in the process of being designed.

The Survey sample application illustrates how you can integrate Microsoft Office and Microsoft Exchange Server applications. For example, a summary of the information collected through the Survey application can be output to Microsoft Word. You can then copy the data into a Microsoft Excel spreadsheet for further analysis or into a Microsoft Word document that can be printed. Because Visual Basic and Microsoft Office applications use the same engine to build custom solutions, you can take advantage of the strengths of each application and programming interface.

If you want to build a customized application closely tied to Microsoft Exchange Server, you can use the *Messaging Application Programming Interface (MAPI) Programmer's Reference* to integrate your applications with Microsoft Exchange Server or to build a custom gateway. You can tailor the Microsoft Exchange Client interface to meet your specific needs, add functionality to the administrative module, or access virtually any portion of the Microsoft Exchange Server infrastructure.

Microsoft Exchange Server provides a broad and readily defined infrastructure, including support for connectivity to the Internet and X.400 systems, as well as a powerful development kit upon which to build the custom applications you need.

Two Case Studies

The best way to learn about the application design capabilities in Microsoft Exchange Server is to see how organizations can apply them. The following scenarios illustrate how two fictitious companies use these capabilities.

Fabrikam, Inc.: Using the Core Functionality in Microsoft Exchange Server

Fabrikam, Inc. is a multinational company with branch sites throughout the world. It has been running a host-based system as its primary internal e-mail system, although some branches have implemented local area network (LAN)-based e-mail in response to user requests.

A reengineering effort has made it apparent to upper management that to reduce administrative, support, training, and custom-development costs, the company will eventually need to standardize on a single e-mail system. E-mail is considered mission-critical because it is relied on heavily by internal users to transfer information.

In addition, users of the company's LAN-based messaging systems frequently send rich-text objects, such as documents and spreadsheets, and are frustrated with the current messaging environment because it does not enable them to share that information with several branches of the company. And, although users have many good ideas for automating processes by using the messaging infrastructure, the IS department often lacks the ability to create them because of the heterogeneous messaging environments, the difficulty in programming applications on their existing messaging system, and a corresponding lack of resources.

Recommendations

The reengineering effort has produced several key recommendations, including:

- **Take advantage of the messaging infrastructure for groupware applications.** The best way to meet cost and functionality objectives is to build groupware applications on a messaging system capable of serving as a mission-critical infrastructure.

- **Use distributed information effectively.** The company believes it is important to have an information infrastructure that will enable it to expand on the capabilities of LAN-based messaging systems. This can be accomplished by making the information available where users need it and can interact with it.

- **Empower end users.** An organization's messaging system needs to empower end users, making it easy for them to find the information they need and to create the applications that enable them to solve business problems.

After conducting a comprehensive review of a variety of products, Fabrikam, Inc. chose Microsoft Exchange Server as its messaging and workgroup platform. In addition to offering strong messaging, connectivity, and administrative capabilities, Microsoft Exchange Server was selected because it includes built-in groupware and supports building additional groupware applications on top of its messaging system, which can handle the mission-critical demands placed upon it.

Leveraging the Messaging Infrastructure for Groupware Applications

Microsoft Exchange Server provides the functionality required for the following types of groupware applications used by Fabrikam, Inc.:

- **Person-to-person routing applications.** Although the company's host-based messaging systems don't support this capability, users of the company's LAN-based system want to use e-mail for routing documents, spreadsheets, and other types of files. This capability, and the frequent need to include other structured information with an attachment (such as forwarding a budget forecast spreadsheet to a vice president, who might then expose information from the spreadsheet as a viewable field in a form), make the creation and routing of point-to-point forms an important capability.

- **Bulletin board applications.** A bulletin board can eliminate the usual difficulties associated with storing information in a file system and can automate and provide ready access to that information. Users no longer have to remember a multitude of network paths or passwords to find information. A variety of object types can be stored, including e-mail messages, documents, spreadsheets, slide presentations, and even voice-mail files. The user has a much broader set of options for viewing and finding files that contain OLE custom properties, because the properties can be made visible in the client view.

- **Discussion area (public folder) applications.** Discussion areas enable users to participate in discussions in easily identifiable locations, rather than through e-mail, as is currently done at Fabrikam, Inc. It also eliminates the problem of trying to keep track of e-mail threads in end users' Inboxes.

- **Tracking applications.** In a workgroup tracking application, users can combine the capabilities of bulletin boards and threaded conversations to create applications that help a group of people collaborate and share information. For instance, a customer-tracking application can enable a sales force to gather the latest information on a potential customer they plan to call on. After the call, the sales force can post information about the call, as well as outstanding customer issues, correspondence, and so on. This capability enables the sales force, who are typically connected only intermittently, to have the latest information. It also enables groups of people who are not necessarily in close physical contact to share information.

Using Distribution Information

Microsoft Exchange Server support for multimaster data replication provides Fabrikam, Inc. the benefits of a *distributed information infrastructure*. This structure enables users to share ideas and work as a team to reach decisions, even if they are thousands of miles and many time zones apart. Fabrikam, Inc. plans to use this capability to create public folders that contain process discussion plans and enable each functional unit to participate in discussions on the plans, including how they might be improved. In this way, the company will benefit from the involvement of the people who best understand how to reengineer a process.

Another benefit of replicated information is the minimal administrative overhead required to keep multiple versions up-to-date. This overhead has been a problem with the company's current system, because much of the information the company wanted to distribute worldwide first had to be copied manually to local office servers. This meant working with links that may or may not be functioning, that disconnect in the middle of transmissions, and that cause a variety of other administrative problems.

Enabling End Users to Accomplish More

Users at Fabrikam, Inc. can make decisions more easily because they will be able to quickly access the information they need. This functionality is provided by the Microsoft Exchange Client and Microsoft Exchange Server working together. The server moves the information throughout the organization, while the client provides the ability to search through data to find the necessary information. The ability of the Microsoft Exchange Client to group, sort, and filter information creates intelligent agents for handling tasks, support for group scheduling, and the ability for users to develop custom forms and build custom applications without programming. All make it easier for users to communicate.

Fabrikam, Inc. users will also be able to create applications quickly and easily. For example, a user may find a public folder application and want to make a similar application with only a few changes (such as copying the customer-tracking application, including its forms, rules, and permissions). Because the application is provided as a sample application on the Microsoft Exchange Server compact disc, it can be used as a model to create a public folder for tracking contractors and other suppliers, eliminating the need to create a similar application from scratch.

The purpose of each public folder is similar: to provide a centrally accessible location where information on outside organizations can be kept, and to enable users of the folder to enter information as it is gathered. To accomplish these tasks, Fabrikam, Inc. intends to use Microsoft Exchange Forms Designer, and will install Microsoft Exchange Forms Designer on most of the company's desktops running the Microsoft Exchange Client. However, the administrator will retain the sole ability to distribute applications created by users to the rest of the company, typically after the application has been completely tested.

Results

Microsoft Exchange Server provides an e-mail infrastructure that is capable of handling Fabrikam, Inc. employees scattered across the globe, yet can be centrally managed from a single desktop. By providing built-in groupware applications, Microsoft Exchange Server provides users with the ability to work together more efficiently without incurring the additional infrastructure, end-user training, or administrative costs that a separate infrastructure would require. Finally, users can quickly and easily access the information they need and build applications that they feel are most valuable.

Trey Research: Taking Full Advantage of the Microsoft Exchange Server Programmable Interface

Trey Research is a diversified global financial investment company whose organizations provide personal banking, investment counseling and sales, and financial market and economic analysis for internal and external customers. As with Fabrikam, Inc., this company has chosen to standardize its messaging system on Microsoft Exchange Server for a variety of reasons. Key to its decision is the native X.400 and Internet connectivity in Microsoft Exchange Server. This capability is not only an internal standard—it enables the company to share information with its many international customers and information suppliers.

Another key advantage of Microsoft Exchange Server is its ability to build custom applications that integrate the company's desktop application suite with Microsoft Exchange Server. Management at Trey Research plans to take advantage of the built-in customization ability of Microsoft Exchange Server to provide users with quick access to the information they need and the ability to use their desktop tools to analyze and format the information.

These capabilities will be provided through customized applications, which will enable users to use Microsoft Exchange Server public folders as repositories for status reports or downloaded news feeds, and then output that data to Microsoft Office applications for spreadsheet analysis, graphing, and charting. After the data analysis has been completed, the new statistical information will be placed in a Microsoft Exchange Server public folder accessible only to executives for review and comment. By using the replication facility in Microsoft Exchange Server as a distributed information transport, and by using the Microsoft Exchange Internet Mail Service to connect Microsoft Exchange Server sites, Trey Research will ensure that important information is distributed automatically to its offices worldwide.

Trey Research also plans to use Schedule+ for project scheduling by linking data maintained in public folders, Microsoft Project, and Schedule+. Microsoft Exchange Server can also enable the company to take advantage of its investment in Visual Basic training for their corporate developers.

In short, Trey Research plans to take advantage of the same capabilities that Fabrikam, Inc. found useful, and the following additional application design benefits of Microsoft Exchange Server, including:

- **Scalable tools for application design** — Many of the solutions Trey Research evaluated as possible workgroup and e-mail infrastructures could only support a limited amount of functionality, or required highly skilled and expensive development resources to implement. Now Trey Research has the tools needed to build applications quickly and to enable their internal development staff to customize applications without worrying about exceeding the functionality available through these tools.

- **Native support for Internet standards** — Trey Research can develop applications that gather relevant information from the Internet and distribute it to its other Microsoft Exchange Server sites worldwide, over an Internet backbone.

- **Integration with the Microsoft Office applications suite** — Trey Research wants to make the most of its investment in Office by integrating its groupware and e-mail with desktop applications and by adopting a common programmable interface for the two. As a result, users can work with a familiar interface, even with custom applications. In addition, the company's development staff will have a common tool set and programming interface available in Office applications—Visual Basic and the scripting language of Visual Basic for Applications—to integrate desktop applications into workgroup solutions.

Support for Scalable Application Design

If an application created by an end user becomes popular and can be rolled out to the rest of the company, Trey Research wants its more experienced development teams to be able to further customize the application. This means that the company needs a solution that can meet the dual—and often conflicting—goals of enabling users to design applications and forms, and enabling the development staff to make those applications more robust, to integrate them with existing applications, or to add additional functionality. Microsoft Exchange Server was the only workgroup and messaging product evaluated by Trey Research that could provide a scalable application design environment.

After an application is rolled out, users inevitably find ways to improve it, and the competitive environment may require additional customizability. Because forms can be customized with Visual Basic, the desired functionality can be added to Microsoft Exchange Server workgroup solutions that use forms. And, because Visual Basic is a powerful programming language capable of calling any Windows-based API, there is virtually no limit to the functionality that can be added.

Integrating with Desktop Software

Trey Research chose Microsoft Office largely because of the powerful programmability provided by Visual Basic for Applications and the various OLE Automation interfaces available in each Office application. Because Microsoft Exchange Server provides an OLE Automation server for MAPI that can be accessed from Microsoft Office applications and Visual Basic, integrating the company's applications with Microsoft Exchange Server will enable it to take advantage of its existing investment; build applications quickly; and add, customize, or change applications rapidly.

Microsoft Office applications can also be integrated into workgroup solutions offered by Microsoft Exchange Server. Microsoft Office documents and spreadsheets, for example, can be stored in the Microsoft Exchange Server information store, as well as shared between the Office applications and Microsoft Exchange Server.

Trey Research plans to use Microsoft Excel as a reporting mechanism for public folder applications. It will be used by the sales managers to automatically compile periodic contact and sales data. For example, a sales representative can enter information on new customers, outstanding customer issues, and sales closed. A sales manager can use the analysis and charting capabilities of Microsoft Excel to evaluate trends and track the business; and then automate the compiling, publication, and distribution of a report by using Microsoft Word and Microsoft Exchange Server.

Results

By investing in a common technology, Trey Research provides key benefits for its users and developers. Sales managers, for example, are familiar with Microsoft Excel as a data-analysis tool. By integrating Microsoft Exchange Server applications into Microsoft Excel for additional analysis and data manipulation, Trey Research's managers don't have to learn a new tool or interface to conduct their analysis.

Summary

Microsoft Exchange Server provides an application design environment that is ideal for rapidly changing business requirements. It enables all users, from novices to skilled programmers, to create custom applications to improve efficiency and make it easier to communicate. It provides a scalable design environment that makes it easy to modify those applications quickly and cost effectively. It also offers reliable, versatile options for connecting to the Internet and X.400 systems to distribute those applications to users virtually anywhere.

Note The names of companies, products, people, characters, and/or data mentioned herein are fictitious and are in no way intended to represent any real individual, company, product, or event, unless otherwise noted.

C H A P T E R   6

Microsoft Exchange Server Registry Reference

This chapter identifies the Registry entries that you can add or change using the Registry Editor. Wherever possible, you should use the Control Panel and the applications in the Windows NT Administrative Tools program group to make changes to the system configuration.

Microsoft Exchange Server Administrator Program Registry Reference

This section provides details on the registry settings used by the Microsoft Exchange Server Administrator program.

CAUTION You should not change any of the Microsoft Exchange Server registry key values unless you are familiar with the full effect of the change.

Under Registry Key:
H_KEY_CURRENT_USER/SOFTWARE/Microsoft/Exchange/
MSExchangeAdmin

Name	Type	Default Value	Description
KMPasswordRemember (flag)			Tells the Administrator program to remember or forget the password.
KMPasswordRemember (msec)			Specifies how many milliseconds to remember the password, if the KMPasswordRemember registry key is set to remember.

Under Registry Key:
H_KEY_CURRENT_USER/SOFTWARE/Microsoft/Exchange/
MSExchangeAdmin/Desktop

Name	Type	Default Value	Description
AppFrame			Specifies the Main Frame window size.
Fonts			
LinkMonitorHeader			Specifies the header for the link monitor MDI window.
SaveOnExit			
ShowCmd			Specifies the startup Administrator window size (minimized or maximized).
StatusBar			
PermissionsHeader			Specifies the permissions page columns header.

Under Registry Key:
H_KEY_CURRENT_USER/SOFTWARE/Microsoft/Exchange/
MSExchangeAdmin/Desktop/Window*x*

Name	Type	Default Value	Description
HListSelection			The selected item in the Admin tree control
Homeserver			The server to which this window was connected
MainMapiHeader			The column header information for the MAPI table on the RHS pane (for example, recipients list)
MainXDSHeader			The header information for the non-MAPI table on the RHS (for example, List of connectors)
SplitterBarPosn			The splitter bar that separates the tree control and the VLB
WindowPlacement			MDI child placement
WindowType			The type of MDI child (monitor or main explorer window)
MonitorName			The DN of the monitor that is run in this window (only for monitor MDI child windows)

Under Registry Key:
H_KEY_CURRENT_USER/SOFTWARE/Microsoft/Exchange/
MSExchangeAdmin/DefaultBrowseDialogDir

Name	Type	Default Value	Description
ImportFile			
ExportFile			
MonitorLog			
EscalationProcess			

Under Registry Key:
H_KEY_CURRENT_USER/SOFTWARE/Microsoft/Exchange/
MSExchangeAdmin/MostRecentlyUsed/MRUx

Name	Type	Default Value	Description
HlistSelection			The selected item in the Admin tree control
HomeServer			The server to which this window was connected to
MainMapiHeader			The column header information for the MAPI table on the RHS pane (such as recipients list)
MainXDSHeader			The header information for the non-MAPI table on the RHS (such as List of connectors)
SplitterPosition			Specifies the location of the splitter bar that separates the tree control and the VLB.
WindowPlacement			MDI child placement
WindowType			The type of MDI child (monitor or main explorer window)
MonitorName			The DN of the monitor that is run in this window (only for monitor MDI child windows)

Under Registry Key:
H_KEY_CURRENT_USER/SOFTWARE/Microsoft/Exchange/
MSExchangeAdmin/FYI

Name	Type	Default Value	Description
NotificationOnNextPass			Specifies whether or not the Administrator program warns about monitor notifications being delayed until next polling pass or immediately.

Under Registry Key:
H_KEY_CURRENT_USER/SOFTWARE/Microsoft/Exchange/
MSExchangeAdminCommon

Name	Type	Default Value	Description
Options			Tools Options Setting, common to Administrator and Mailumx Directory structure doc

Microsoft Exchange Server Directory Structure

Setup creates the default directory structure shown here when all components are installed. Note where setup creates shared directories. The directory structure shown here is the default structure if all components are installed with the default values. General Microsoft Exchange Server and Administrator program files are in the \Exchsrvr directory.

Note If you specify a separate directory for the Administrator program, the files that are common to both the Administrator program and Microsoft Exchange Server are duplicated in the \Exchsrvr directory and in the directory you specified for the Administrator program. The files installed in these directories are listed below.

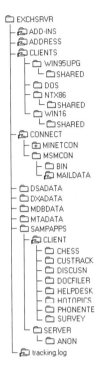

```
EXCHSRVR
├─ ADD-INS
├─ ADDRESS
├─ CLIENTS
│      ├─ WIN95UPG
│      │      └─ SHARED
│      ├─ DOS
│      ├─ NTX86
│      │      └─ SHARED
│      └─ WIN16
│             └─ SHARED
├─ CONNECT
│      ├─ MINETCON
│      └─ MSMCON
│             ├─ BIN
│             └─ MAILDATA
├─ DSADATA
├─ DXADATA
├─ MDBDATA
├─ MTADATA
├─ SAMPAPPS
│      ├─ CLIENT
│      │      ├─ CHESS
│      │      ├─ CUSTRACK
│      │      ├─ DISCUSN
│      │      ├─ DOCFILER
│      │      ├─ HELPDESK
│      │      ├─ HOTOPICS
│      │      ├─ PHONENTE
│      │      └─ SURVEY
│      └─ SERVER
│             └─ ANON
└─ tracking.log
```

Microsoft Exchange Server Client Files

The files installed depend on the version selected.

- Windows 95 Client
- DOS Client
- Windows NT Client
- Windows 3.1 or Windows for Workgroups Client

Microsoft Exchange Server Files

- Setup program
- Administrator program
- Microsoft Exchange Server
- Shared files

Microsoft Windows 95 Client Files

Installed In: CLIENT\WIN95UPG	Installed In: CLIENT\WIN95UPG\SHARED
ACMSETUP.EXE	MSINFO.EXE
ACMSETUP.HLP	MSSP232.DLL
ADMIN.INF	MSSP2_EN.LEX
APNAME.LST	
APPXEC32.DLL	
AV41206.FMT	
AV41256.FMT	
AV41307.FMT	
AV41357.FMT	
BOOMERR.TXT	
BOOMHELP.TXT	
CAN32.CFG	
CARD1.PRT	
CBTLIB4.DLL	
CMC.DLL	
CNFNOT.CFG	
CNFNOT.ICO	
CNFNOT32.EXE	
CNFRES.CFG	
COMDLG16.OCX	
CONFLICT.ICO	
CTL3D3_.DLL	
CTL3DV_.DLL	
CUECARD.HLP	
DATAZAP.DLL	
DATZAP16.DLL	
DATZAP32.DLL	
DAY1.PRT	
DAY2.PRT	
DYNO106.FMT	

(continued)

Installed In: CLIENT\WIN95UPG	Installed In: CLIENT\WIN95UPG\SHARED
EMSABP32.DLL	
EMSUI32.DBG	
EMSUI32.DLL	
EMSUIX32.DBG	
EMSUIX32.DLL	
ETEXCH32.DLL	
EXCHNG.CNT	
EXCHNG.HLP	
EXCHNG.INF	
EXCHGN.LES	
EXCHNG.STF	
EXCHGN32.DBG	
EXCHGN32.EXE	
FORMCOM.HLP	
ILECOMM.DLL	
ILREM.DLL	
ILS.EXM	
ILS.STR	
ILX9600.FIL	
ILXACT.FIL	
ILXECCO.FIL	
ILXHP95.FIL	
ILXLATE.EXE	
ILXLATE.HLP	
ILXMSA.FIL	
ILXORG.FIL	
ILXRAT.FIL	
ILXSHARP.FIL	
ILXSPL2.FIL	
ILXW.DLL	
ILXWPAD.FIL	
MAIL.PRT	

(continued)

Installed In: **CLIENT\WIN95UPG**	Installed In: **CLIENT\WIN95UPG\SHARED**
MAPI.DLL	
MAPI32.DBG	
MAPI32.DLL	
MAPIF0.CFG	
MAPIF0L.ICO	
MAPIF0S.ICO	
MAPIF1.CFG	
MAPIF10.CFG	
MAPIF11.CFG	
MAPIF11L.ICO	
MAPIF11S.ICO	
MAPIF1L.ICO	
MAPIF1S.ICO	
MAPIF2.CFG	
MAPIF2L.ICO	
MAPIF2S.ICO	
MAPIF3.CFG	
MAPIF3L.ICO	
MAPIF3S.ICO	
MAPIF4.CFG	
MAPIF4L.ICO	
MAPIF4S.ICO	
MAPIF5.CFG	
MAPIF5L.ICO	
MAPIF5S.ICO	
MAPIF6.CFG	
MAPIF6L.ICO	
MAPIF6S.ICO	
MAPIF7.CFG	
MAPIF7L.ICO	
MAPIF7S.ICO	
MAPIF8.CFG	
MAPIF8L.ICO	

(continued)

Installed In: CLIENT\WIN95UPG	Installed In: CLIENT\WIN95UPG\SHARED
MAPIF8S.ICO	
MAPIF9.CFG	
PAPIFORM.VBX	
MAPIFVBX.REG	
MAPIRPC.REG	
MAPIFSP32.DBG	
MAPISP32.EXE	
MAPISRVR.EXE	
MAPISVC.INF	
MC.ICO	
MCS.ICO	
MDISP.EXE	
MDISP.REG	
MDISP.TLB	
MEFLIB.DLL	
MENUSEL.VBX	
ML3XEC16.EXE	
MLCFG32.CPL	
MLCFG32.DBG	
MLCTRL.DLL	
MLSET32.EXE	
MLSETP32.DBG	
MLSETP32.DLL	
MMFMIG32.DLL	
MONTH1.PRT	
MR.ICO	
MRN.ICO	
MRP.ICO	
MRPS.ICO	
MRS.ICO	
MRT.ICO	
MRTS.ICO	
MSCAL32.DLL	

(continued)

Installed In: CLIENT\WIN95UPG	Installed In: CLIENT\WIN95UPG\SHARED
MSCALL16.OCX	
MSCPYDIS.DLL	
MSFS.CNT	
MSFS.HLP	
SMFS32.DBG	
MSFS32.DLL	
MSPST32.DBG	
MSPST32.DLL	
MSRICHED.VBX	
MSSCD32.DLL	
MSSETUP.DLL	
MSSPC32.DLL	
MSTABCTL.VBX	
MSTRE32.DLL	
MSTRS32.DLL	
MSVCRT20.DLL	
NORMAL.FMT	
OC25.DLL	
PLAY.EXE	
README.TXT	
ERGOCX16.EXE	
REQ32.CFG	
RICHED.DLL	
RICHED32.DBG	
RICHED32.DLL	
RPN32.CFG	
RPP32.CFG	
RPT32.CFG	
SCANPST.HLP	
SCHDPL32.EXE	
SCHDPLUS.CNT	
SCHDPLUS.HLP	
SCHDPLUS.LES	

(continued)

Installed In: CLIENT\WIN95UPG	Installed In: CLIENT\WIN95UPG\SHARED
SECURE.CFG	
SECURL.ICO	
SECURS.ICO	
SETUP.EXE	
SETUP.INI	
SETUP.LST	
SIGN.CFG	
SIGNLRG.ICO	
SIGNSM.ICO	
SPIN16.OCX	
SPUS_BB.DLL	
TABLES.ITB	
TASK1.PRT	
TASK2.PRT	
TASK3.PRT	
TEXT1.PRT	
THREED16.OCX	
TRIFOLD3.PRT	
VAEN2.DLL	
VAEN2.OLB	
VB40016.DLL	
VB4EN16.DLL	
VB4STP32.DLL	
VLB.DLL	
VLB32.DLL	
WEEK1.RPT	
WEEK2.RPT	
WMSFR.DLL	
WMSFR32.DBG	
WMSFR32.DLL	
WMSUI.DLL	
WMSUI32.DBG	
WMSUI32.DLL	

(continued)

DOS Client Files

Installed In: CLIENT\DOS	Installed In: CLIENT\NTX86\SHARED
_MSSETUP.EXE	
CONNECT.EXE	MSINFO.EXE
CONNECT.HLP	MSSP232.DLL
DIALNDIS.EXE	MSSP2_EN.LEX
DIALODI.EXE	
EXCHANGE.EXE	
EXDCHANGE.HLP	
MLSETUP.INI	
MODEMS.INI	
README.TXT	
RPC16C1.RPC	
RPC16C3.RPC	
RPC16C4.RPC	
RPC16C5.RPC	
RPC16C6.RPC	
RPC16DG3.RPC	
RPC16DG6.RPC	
PRCNS.RPC	
RPCNSLM.RPC	
RPCNSMGM.RPC	
SECURITY.RPC	
SETUP.EXE	
SETUP.INF	

Windows NT Client Files

Installed In: CLIENT\NTX86
ACMSETUP.EXE
ACMSETUP.HLP
ADMIN.INF
APNAME.LST
APPXEC32.DLL
AV41206.FMT

(continued)

Installed In: CLIENT\NTX86

AV41256.FMT

AV41307.FMT

AV41357.FMT

BOOMERR.TXT

BOOMHELP.TXT

CAN32.CFG

CARD1.PRT

CBTLIB4.DLL

CMC.DLL

CNFNOT.CFG

CNFNOT32.EXE

CNFRES.CFG

COMDLG16.OCX

CONFICT.ICO

CTL3D3_.DLL

CTL3DV_.DLL

CUECARD.HLP

DATAZAP.DLL

DATZAP16.DLL

DATZAP32.DLL

DAY1.PRT

DAY2.PRT

DYNO106.FMT

EMSABP32.DLL

EMSMDB32.DLL

EMSUI32.DBG

EMSUI32.DLL

EMSUIX32.DLL

ETEXCH32.DLL

EXCFG32.EXE

EXCHNG.CNT

EXCHNG.HLP

EXCHNG.INF

EXCHNG.LES

(continued)

Installed In: CLIENT\NTX86

EXCHNG.STF

EXCHNG32.DBG

EXCHNG32.EXE

FAXVIEW.EXE

FORMCOM.HLP

ILECOMM.DLL

ILREM.DLL

ILS.EXM

ILS.STR

ILX9600.FIL

ILXACT.FIL

ILXECCO.FIL

ILXORG.FIL

ILXRAT.FIL

ILXSHARP.FIL

ILXSPL2.FIL

ILXW.DLL

ILXWPAD.FIL

MAIL.PRT

MAPI.DLL

MAPI32.DBG

MAPI32.DLL

MAPIF0.CFG

MAPIF0L.ICO

MAPIF0S.ICO

MAPIF1.CFG

MAPIF10.CFG

MAPIF11.CFG

MAPIF11L.ICO

MAPIF11S.ICO

MAPIF1L.ICO

MAPIF1S.ICO

MAPIF2.CFG

MAPIF2L.ICO

(continued)

Installed In: CLIENT\NTX86

MAPIF2S.ICO

MAPIF3.CFG

MAPIF3L.ICO

MAPIF3S.ICO

MAPIF4.CFG

MAPIF4L.ICO

MAPIF4S.ICO

MAPIF5.CFG

MAPIF5L.ICO

MAPIF5S.ICO

MAPIF6.CFG

MAPIF6L.ICO

MAPIF6S.ICO

MAPIF7.CFG

MAPIF7L.ICO

MAPIF7S.ICO

MAPIF8.CFG

MAPIF8L.ICO

MAPIF8S.ICO

MAPIF9.CFG

MAPIFORM.VBX

MAPIFVBX.REG

MAPIFVBX.TLB

MAPIRPC.REG

MAPISP32.DBG

MAPISP32.EXE

MAPISRVR.EXE

MAPISVC.INF

MC.ICO

MCS.ICO

MDISP.EXE

MDISP.REG

MDISP.TLB

MEFLIB.DLL

(continued)

Installed In: CLIENT\NTX86

MENUSEL.VBX

MHCOMD.VBX

ML3XEC16.EXE

MLCFG32.CPL

MLCFG32.DBG

MLCTRL.DLL

MLSETP32.DBG

MLSETP32.DLL

MMFMIG32.DLL

MONTH1.PRT

MR.ICO

MRN.ICO

MRNS.ICO

MRP.ICO

MRPS.ICO

MRS.ICO

MRT.ICO

MRTS.ICO

MSCAL32.DLL

MSCALL16.OCX

MSCPYDIS.DLL

MSFS.HLP

MSFS32.DBG

MSPST32.DLL

MSRICHED.VBX

MSSCD32.DLL

MSSETUP.DLL

MSTABCTL.VBX

MSTRE32.DLL

MSTRS32.DLL

MSVCRT20.DLL

NORMAL.FMT

OC25.DLL

PLAY.EXE

(continued)

Installed In: CLIENT\NTX86

README.TXT

REGOCX16.EXE

REQ32.CFG

RICHED.DLL

RICHED32.DBG

RICHED32.DLL

RPN32.CFG

RPP32.CFG

RPT32.CFG

SCHDPL32.EXE

SCHDPLUS.HLP

SCHDPLUS.LES

SECURE.CFG

SECURL.ICO

SECURS.ICO

SETUP.EXE

SETUP.INI

SETUP.LST

SIGN.CFG

SIGNLRG.ICO

SIGNSM.ICO

SPIN16.OCX

SPLUS_BB.DLL

TABLES.ITB

TASK1.PRT

TASK2.PRT

TASK3.PRT

TEXT1.PRT

THREED16.OCX

TRIFOLD3.PRT

VAEN2.DLL

VAEN2.OLB

VB40016.DLL

VB4EN16.DLL

(continued)

Installed In: CLIENT\NTX86

VB4STP32.DLL

VLB.DLL

VLB32.DBG

VLB32.DLL

WEEK1.RPT

WEEK2.RPT

WMSFR.DLL

WMSUI.DLL

WMSUI32.DBG

WMSUI32.DLL

_MSSETUP.EXE

Windows 3.1 or Windows for Workgroups Client Files

Installed In: CLIENT\WIN16

ACMSETUP.EXE

ACMSETUP.HLP

ADMIN.INF

APNAME.LST

APPXEC32.DLL

AV41206.FMT

AV41256.FMT

AV41307.FMT

AV41357.FMT

BOOMERR.TXT

BOOMHELP.TXT

CALLIN.BAT

CAN16.CFG

CARD1.PRT

CBTLIB4.DLL

CMC.DLL

CNFNOT.CFG

CNFNOT.EXE

(continued)

Installed In: CLIENT\WIN16

CNFRES.CFG

COMDLG16.OCX

COMPDRV.EXE

COMPOBJ.DLL

CONFIG.HLP

CONFIG.TXT

CONFLICT.ICO

CONNAPI.DLL

CONNECT.EX_

CONNECT.HLP

CONNECTW.EX_

CONNECTW.HLP

CTL3D.DLL

CTL3DV.DLL

CUECARD.HLP

DATAZAP.DLL

DAY1.PRT

DAY2.PRT

DEMILAYR.DLL

DIAL.386

DIALCOMP.EXE

DIALNDIS.EXE

DIALODI.EXE

DISPDIB.DLL

DWSPYDLL.DLL

DYNO106.FMT

EMSABP.DLL

EMSMDB.DLL

EMSUI.DLL

EMSUIX.DLL

ETEXCH.DLL

EXCFG.EXE

EXCHNG.EXE

EXCHNG.HLP

(continued)

Installed In: CLIENT\WIN16

EXCHNG.INF

EXCHNG.LES

EXCHNG.STF

FAXVIEW.EXE

FORMCOM.HLP

GUARD.EXE

HANGUP.BAT

ILECOMM.DLL

ILREM.DLL

ILS.EXM

ILS.STR

ILX9600.FIL

ILXACT.FIL

ILXECCO.FIL

ILXHP95.FIL

ILXLATE.EXE

ILXLATE.HLP

ILXMSA.FIL

ILXORG.FIL

ILXRAT.FIL

ILXSHARP.FIL

ILXSPL2.FIL

ILXW.DLL

ILXWPAD.FIL

MAIL.PRT

MAILMGR.DLL

MAPI.DLL

MAPIF0.CFG

MAPIF0L.ICO

MAPIF0S.ICO

MAPIF1.CFG

MAPIF10.CFG

MAPIF11.CFG

MAPIF11L.ICO

(continued)

Installed In: CLIENT\WIN16

MAPIF11S.ICO

MAPIF1L.ICO

MAPIF1S.ICO

MAPIF2.CFG

MAPIF2L.ICO

MAPIF2S.ICO

MAPIF3.CFG

MAPIF3L.ICO

MAPIF3S.ICO

MAPIF4.CFG

MAPIF4L.ICO

MAPIF4S.ICO

MAPIF5.CFG

MAPIF5L.ICO

MAPIF5S.ICO

MAPIF6.CFG

MAPIF6L.ICO

MAPIF6S.ICO

MAPIF7.CFG

MAPIF7L.ICO

MAPIF7S.ICO

MAPIF8.CFG

MAPIF8L.ICO

MAPIF8S.ICO

MAPIF9.CFG

PAPIFORM.VBX

MAPIFVBX.REG

MAPIRPC.REG

MAPISP.EXE

MAPISVC.INF

MC.ICO

MCS.ICO

MDISP.EXE

MDISP.REG

(continued)

Installed In: CLIENT\WIN16

MDISP.TLB

MEFLIB.DLL

MENUSEL.VBX

MLCFG.DLL

MLCTRL.DLL

Microsoft Exchange Server Information Store Registry Key Structure

The following diagram shows the keys created in the registry when information store is installed by Microsoft Exchange Server Setup.

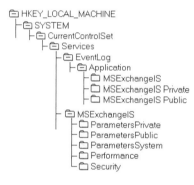

Microsoft Exchange Server Information Store Registry Reference

This section provides the details on the registry settings used by the Information Store. Values that are shown bold are created by Server Setup. Values that are not bold are not visible until you create them. If you do not specify a value, the default value is used. If you specify a value that is outside the minimum or maximum value, the maximum or minimum is used, respectively.

- Key Structure
- Key/Value Hierarchy

Caution   You should not change any of the Microsoft Exchange Server registry key values unless you are familiar with the full effect of the change.

Under Registry Key:
SYSTEM\CURRENTCONTROLSET\SERVICES\MSEXCHANGEIS\
PARAMETERSSYSTEM

Name	Type	Default Value	Description
Aging Clean Interval		900	**Units:** Seconds **Min:** 60 **Max:** 3600 Column Aging and Index Aging occurs during the Maintenance Schedule set in Administrator on the server object. This interval indicates how long to wait after the start of a clean before starting another clean. If the clean takes longer than this interval, a new clean is started immediately after the first clean completes.
Aging Keep Time		900	**Units:** Seconds **Min:** 60 **Max:** 3600 Column Aging and Index Aging occurs during the Maintenance Schedule set in Administrator on the server object. This interval indicates how long to keep columns of indices before they are cleaned.
Circular Logging			Whether to use Jet circular logging. This causes transaction log files to be reused. When this is on, differential and incremental backups will not work. The information store service must be restarted to reread this value after it is toggled.
DB Log Path			Where Edb*.log files go
DB Recovery			Whether to activate logging/recovery. 0 = no, 1 = yes.

(continued)

Name	Type	Default Value	Description
DB System Path			Path where System.edb is located.
DS Computer			Server where the DS to use is located
Max Threads			Maximum number of threads that are created by the information store service.
MTA Computer			Server where the MTA to use is located
Online Compaction			On or off
Reread GWART Interval		900	**Units:** Seconds **Min:** 60 **Max:** 3600 The interval at which the GWART is reread so that new gateways can be detected.
Reread Information Store Quotas Interval		900	**Units:** Seconds **Min:** 60 **Max:** 3600 The interval at which quotas on the information store object in the DS are read in order to update.
Synch Mailbox/Check OOF Interval		900	**Units:** Seconds **Min:** 60 **Max:** 3600
This Server			Name of this server
Working Directory			Path to working directory for information store

Under Registry Key:
System\CurrentControlSet\Services\MSExchangeIS\ParametersPrivate

Name	Type	Default Value	Description
Clean Per User Read Interval		900	**Units:** Seconds
			Min: 60
			Max: 3600
			Cleaning per user read occurs during the Maintenance Schedule set in Administrator on the server object. This interval indicates how long to wait after the start of a clean before starting another clean. If the clean takes longer than this interval, a new clean is started immediately after the first clean completes.
DB Path			Path where Expriv.eis is located.
Disabled			Disables the Private store. 0 = Not disabled. 1 = Disabled.
General Event Log			Mask used to control which sub-categories within each event log category are actually written to the NT event log. Its default value is 0. This will cause a few very basic (start and stop) events to be logged. Set mask to 0xFFFFFFFF to log all events.
Log Downloads			Bit mask to control which download actions (items copied out of the information store) are written to the event log. Normally set to 0 (default) for the Private information store.
			Bits:
			0x1 Attachment downloads
			0x2 Message downloads
			0x4 Folder downloads

(continued)

Name	Type	Default Value	Description
Reread Logon Quotas Interval		900	**Units:** Seconds **Min:** 60 **Max:** 3600 This interval indicates how often to read logon object quotas from the DS.
Track Duplicates		1	**Units:** Hours **Min:** 1 **Max:** 24 Time interval for which duplicates are tracked at delivery. This is the interval for which information on received messages will be kept and duplicates will be eliminated. The BackgroundCleanup task must be enabled for this to work.
Transport Event Log			See Private General Event Log

Under Registry Key: System\CurrentControlSet\Services\MSExchangeIS\ParametersPublic

Name	Type	Default Value	Description
DB Path			Path where Expub.eis is located.
Disabled			Disables the Public store. 0 = Not disabled. 1 = Disabled.
General Event Log			Mask used to control which sub-categories within each event log category are actually written to the NT event log. This will cause a few very basic (start and stop) events to be logged. Set mask to 0xFFFFFFFF to log all events.

(continued)

Name	Type	Default Value	Description
Log Downloads			Bit mask to control which download actions (items copied out of the information store) are written to the event log.
			Bits:
			0x1 Attachment downloads
			0x2 Message downloads
			0x4 Folder downloads
Maximum Cached Categorizations			
Read PF Instances Interval		900	**Units:** Seconds
			Min: 60
			Max: 3600
			This interval indicates how often to read the DS to determine which public folders are replicated to this server.
Read PF Settings Interval		900	**Units:** Seconds
			Min: 60
			Max: 3600
			This interval indicates how often to read the DS to determine the replication configuration of public folders that are replicated to this server.
			Replication has 3 possible values (the default value is 1):
			0: replication disabled
			1: replication enabled, with default settings (registry overrides are ignored)
			2: replication enabled, using registry overrides, if they are available.
			Replication Backfill Timeout (Solicited): Timeout value used for testing backfill. Don't change the default value.

(continued)

Name	Type	Default Value	Description
			Replication Backfill Timeout (Unsolicited): Timeout value used for testing backfill. Don't change the default value.
		900	Replication DS Updates
			Units: Seconds
			Min: 900
			Max: 3600
			This is the time interval at which the replication agent will look for updates from the directory service. This requires a DS call for every folder in the IPM subfolder tree, and the DS calls are very slow right now (up to 20 seconds per call), so don't set this value too small.
Replication Event Log			This is a 32-bit mask of the replication sub-categories used when writing to the Windows NT event log (application). Enabling the appropriate bits listed below will enable detailed information about various specific areas of replication. It is intended primarily for debug use, but will ship as part of the product, to help track down problems in the field.
			// equivalent to TraceError - will list every function and its error code returned
			#define elscLogError (ELSC)0x80000000
			// report high level replication errors
			#define elscReplError (ELSC)0x00000001
			// report changes from the directory service
			#define elscReplDs (ELSC)0x00000002
			// report information related to incoming replication messages
			#define elscReplMsgIn (ELSC)0x00000004
			// report information on outgoing replication messages
			#define elscReplMsgOut (ELSC)0x00000008

(continued)

Name	Type	Default Value	Description
Replication Event Log (cont.)			// report information on the MDBs to which a replication message is mailed
			#define elscReplMsgOutRecipients (ELSC)0x00000010
			// report information on replication conflicts, and their resolution
			#define elscReplConflict (ELSC)0x00000020
			// report information on replication message timeouts
			#define elscReplTimeout (ELSC)0x00000040
			// report information on message expiration by age limit from public folders
			#define elscReplExpiry (ELSC)0x00000080
			This default setting is 0, which will cause only the replication agent start and stop to be written to the Windows NT event log. The other subcategories are subject to change without notice, as is the format of the entries in the event log. Additional subcategories will be added in the future. If you want to see all of the possible replication category event log entries, set the "Replication Event Log" value to 0xFFFFFFFF. You need a lot of disk space for this.
Replication Expiry		900	**Units:** Seconds
			Min: 60
			Max: 3600
			Messages are expired during the Maintenance Schedule set in Administrator on the server object. This interval indicates how long to wait after the start of the last expiry before starting another expiry. If the expiry takes longer than this interval, a new expiry is started immediately after the first expiry completes.

(continued)

Name	Type	Default Value	Description
Replication Folder Count Limit		10	Because public folders are slow to create, transport replication message size limits and internal size limits, it is necessary to place a folder count limit (per replication message). If 20 folders have been created but not yet replicated, and the "Replication Folder Count Limit" is set to 10, then the first 10 folders will be sent in 1 replication message, immediately followed by the next 10 in another replication message.
Replication Message Count Limit		20	Same as Replication Folder Count Limit, but for messages.
Replication RMR Timeout		3600	**Units:** Seconds **Min:** 60 **Max:** 3600 This is the time interval that replication messages which cannot be processed will be held.
Replication Send Folder Tree		60	**Units:** Seconds **Min:** 60 **Max:** 3600 Used to override the default rate at which the folder hierarchy is replicated.
Replication Status Updates		3600	**Units:** Seconds **Min:** 60 **Max:** 3600 Time interval at which status broadcasts will be sent for a folder. When this much time has passed with no replication messages sent for a given folder, a status message will automatically be sent.

(continued)

Name	Type	Default Value	Description
Replication Timeout		60	**Units:** Seconds
			Min: 60
			Max: 900
			This is the frequency at which the replication agent will check its internal state tables for backfill timeouts. Smaller values will cause timeouts to be detected closer to the actual timeout, but also tend to swamp the server. Don't change the default value unless you know what you are doing.
Track Duplicates		1	**Units:** Hours
			Min: 1
			Max: 24
			Time interval for which duplicates are tracked at delivery. This is the number of hours for which information on received messages will be kept and duplicates will be eliminated. The BackgroundCleanup task must be enabled for this to work.
Transport Event Log			See Public General Event Log.

Under Registry Key:
System\CurrentControlSet\Services\EventLog\Application\MSExchangeIS

Name	Type	Default Value	Description
CategoryCount			Specifies the number of categories supported.
CategoryMessage File			Specifies the path and filename for the category message file.
EventMessageFile			Specifies the path and filename for the event identifier message file.

Under Registry Key:
System\CurrentControlSet\Services\EventLog\Application
MSExchangeIS Private

Name	Type	Default Value	Description
CategoryCount			Specifies the number of categories supported.
CategoryMessage File			Specifies the path and filename for the category message file.
EventMessageFile			Specifies the path and filename for the event identifier message file.

Under Registry Key:
System\CurrentControlSet\Services\EventLog\Application\MSExchangeIS
Public

Name	Type	Default Value	Description
CategoryCount			Specifies the number of categories supported.
CategoryMessage File			Specifies the path and filename for the category message file.
EventMessageFile			Specifies the path and filename for the event identifier message file.

Under Registry Key:
System\CurrentControlSet\Services\MSExchangeIS

Name	Type	Default Value	Description
DependOnGroup			The Group this service belongs to. For the information store, none.
DependOnService			Services the information store depends on. For the information store, MSExchangeDS.
DisplayName			Long display name of the service. For the information store, Microsoft Exchange Information Store.
ErrorControl			Specifies the severity of the error if the information store fails to start during startup and determines the action taken by the startup program if failure occurs.

(continued)

Name	Type	Default Value	Description
ImagePath			Path to .Exe file for information store service.
ObjectName			Specifies the machine account for the context that the service will be run under.
Start			Specifies when to start the service (autostart, manual start, disabled, etc.)
Type			Specifies the type of service (Win32 process, Windows NT device driver, Windows NT file system driver, etc.)

Under Registry Key:
System\CurrentControlSet\Services\MSExchangeIS\Performance

These are all Performance Monitor settings.

Name	Type	Default Value	Description
Close			
Collect			
First Counter			
First Help			
Last Counter			
Last Help			
Library			
Open			

Under Registry Key:
System\CurrentControlSet\Services\MSExchangeIS\Security

Name	Type	Default Value	Description
Security			

Microsoft Exchange Server Tools and Reference

This section provides access to the following Microsoft Exchange Server online information:

- Windows NT Registry Settings Reference
- File Reference and Directory Structure

Windows NT Registry Settings Reference

This section covers only the Windows NT Registry entries that are added or modified by Microsoft Exchange Server.

Caution   Most of the Microsoft Exchange Server registry key values should not be changed by editing the registry. Use this section for information only. If manual editing is supported, the registry entry is bolded and "Can Edit" is noted in the file.

Example:

If you have this registry key:

```
HKEY_LOCAL_MACHINE\SYSTEM\CurrentControlSet\Services\MSExchangeIMC
\Parameters\<parameter>
```

You would specify the BadInMessageAction parameter for this registry key as follows, on one line:

```
HKEY_LOCAL_MACHINE\SYSTEM\CurrentControlSet\Services\MSExchangeIMC
\Parameters\BadInMessageAction = 1
```

For information on finding and editing keys in the registry or using the Registry Editor, see the *Windows NT Resource Guide*.

File Reference and Directory Structure

This section describes the files and directory structure that Microsoft Exchange Server installs during setup.

- Directory Structure
- File Reference

Microsoft Exchange Server MTA Registry Reference

This section describes how configuration information from the Windows NT Registry is used by the Microsoft Exchange Server message transfer agent (MTA).

This section includes those registry parameters that are created by Microsoft Exchange Server Setup and those that can be manually added later for specific functionality. The registry items that are optional and not created by setup are denoted by an asterisk (*) following the name. Registry values with asterisks will not always be found within the MTA Parameters section of the registry. The Registry keys and defaults are all defined in the file Ntil\cc\mtareg.h.

Caution   You should not change any of the Microsoft Exchange Server registry key values unless you are familiar with the full effect of the change.

Under Registry Key:

#Define for KEY	Registry Key Name	Default
SCT_CALL_STACK	"Call-stack diagnostics required"	1
SCT_NCC_TP0_TEST	"NCC TP0 Conformance Tester"	0
SCT_MDB_USERS	"MDB users"	1500
SCT_MMI_CONNS	"MMI connections"	8
SCT_MDB_DEL_Q	"Concurrent MDB/delivery queue clients"	50
SCT_MT_GWY_CLI	"MT gateway clients"	10
SCT_RET_Q_CLI	"Retrieval queue clients"	10
SCT_LMTA_CONNS	"Concurrent connections to LAN-MTAs"	40
SCT_RAS_CONNS	"Concurrent connections to RAS LAN-MTAs"	10
SCT_CONC_LMTAS	"Number of LAN-MTA entities"	20
SCT_X400_GWYS	"Number of X.400 gateway entities"	20
SCT_CLIENT_TCBS	"XAPI/MMI client DMOD threads"	10
SCT_MTA_TCBS	"LAN-MTA DMOD threads"	5
SCT_RAS_TCBS	"RAS LAN-MTA DMOD threads"	2
SCT_TP4_CBS	"TP4 control blocks"	20
SCT_TP4_THDS	"TP4 threads"	2
SCT_TP4_SELECT	"TP4 Async notify timeout (msec)"	100
SCT_RFC_CBS	"TCP/IP control blocks"	20
SCT_RFC_THDS	"TCP/IP threads"	2
SCT_RFC_SELECT	"TCP/IP Async notify timeout (msec)"	100
SCT_XAPI_APPL	"XAPI MA threads"	1
SCT_XAPI_GWAY	"XAPI MT threads"	1

(continued)

#Define for KEY	Registry Key Name	Default
SCT_XAPI_DEL	"XAPI MA queue threads"	1
SCT_XAPI_XFER	"XAPI MT queue threads"	
SCT_XAPI_SESS	"Concurrent XAPI sessions"	100
SCT_MTA_SUB	"Submit/deliver threads"	1
SCT_MTA_DSP	"Dispatcher threads"	1
SCT_MTA_XFER	"Transfer threads"	1
SCT_DS_CACHE	"ds_read cache latency (secs)"	60
SCT_DS_SEARCH	"ds_search latency (mins) for transport stacks"	60
SCT_PLAT_RTS	"RTS threads"	1
SCT_PLAT_KER	"Kernel threads"	1
SCT_OSI_DBUFS	"DB data buffers per object"	5
SCT_OSI_DBFILE	"DB file handles"	64
SCT_X400_SVC_LOG	"X.400 Service Event Log"	0
SCT_EICON_WAIT	"Eicon wait timeout (msec)"	500
SCT_EICON_RESULT	"Eicon X.25 result threads"	2
SCT_EICON_CONNS	"Eicon X.25 connections"	32
SCT_DB_FILECOUNT	"DB file count delete threshold"	0
SCT_DB_FILESIZE	"DB file size delete threshold"	0
SCT_RAMREC_SEV0	"RAM log severity (X.400 Service)"	4
SCT_RAMREC_SEV1	"RAM log severity (Resource)"	4
SCT_RAMREC_SEV2	"RAM log severity (Security)"	4
SCT_RAMREC_SEV3	"RAM log severity (Interface)"	4
SCT_RAMREC_SEV4	"RAM log severity (Field Engineering)"	4
SCT_RAMREC_SEV5	"RAM log severity (Operator event)"	4
SCT_RAMREC_SEV6	"RAM log severity (Configuration)"	4
SCT_RAMREC_SEV7	"RAM log severity (Directory Access)"	4
SCT_RAMREC_SEV8	"RAM log severity (Operating System)"	4
SCT_RAMREC_SEV9	"RAM log severity (Internal Processing)"	4
SCT_LOG_APDUS	"APDU logging required"	0
MTA_DIRNAME_KEY	"X500 DN"	Constructed from setup parameters

(continued)

#Define for KEY	Registry Key Name	Default
DSA_ADDRESS_KEY	"DSA Address"	Constructed from setup parameters
MTA_RUNDIR_KEY	"MTA Run Directory"	Constructed from setup parameters
SCT_SECURE_RSLT	"Flush Results to Disk"	1
SCT_RAS_MTAS	"Number of RAS LAN-MTAs"	10
SCT_LAN_SITES	"Number of remote sites connected over LAN"	25
SCT_MAX_DLS	"Number of DLs allowed"	100
SCT_MAX_XAPI_APPS	"Max concurrent XAPI applications"	10
SCT_MAX_RPC_CALLS	"Max RPC calls outstanding"	50
SCT_MIN_RPC_THREAD	"Min RPC Threads"	4
SCT_RPC_AUTH_LEVEL	"RPC Authentication Level"	2
SCT_REDISPATCH	"Dispatch remote MTA messages"	0
SCT_TEXT_LOG	"Text Event Log"	0
SCT_ENABLE_SEH	"Handle Exceptions"	0
SCT_DB_FILE_PATH	"MTA database path"	Constructed from setup parameters

Registry Key Descriptions

Call-stack diagnostics required

Provides a call stack for each MTA thread at termination time. This option is a performance hit and is only available on the debug MTA.

NCC TP0 Conformance Tester

Binds the MTA TP0 code to the NCC conformance test tool rather than the MTA upper layers, for conformance testing.

MDB users

Maximum number of MDB users supported by the MTA. Users in Microsoft Exchange are MDB users by default unless explicitly set otherwise.

MMI connections

Maximum number of MMI connections to the MTA. Each Administrator instance using the MTA Administrator API uses one MMI connection and is treated as an MMI client.

Concurrent MDB/Delivery Queue clients

Maximum number of MDBs and XAPI MA Delivery Queue clients supported by the MTA. This should be set to at least two to support the Private and Public MDB entities.

MT Gateway clients

Maximum number of XAPI MT Gateway clients supported by the MTA.

Retrieval Queue clients

Maximum number of XAPI MA Retrieval Queue clients supported by the MTA.

Concurrent connections to LAN-MTAs

Maximum number of concurrent connections to MTAs over the LAN. MTAs communicating over the LAN are known as LAN-MTAs.

The local MTA may have multiple connections to a remote MTA depending on configuration and system load.

Concurrent connections to RAS LAN-MTAs

Maximum number of concurrent connections to remote MTAs over RAS.

Number of LAN-MTA entities

Maximum number of LAN-MTAs supported by the MTA.

Number of X.400 gateway entities

Maximum number of remote MTAs connecting via X.400 OSI links (as opposed to connecting over LAN-MTA or RAS). OSI links use X.25, RFC1006(TCP/IP) or TP4.

XAPI/MMI client DMOD threads

Maximum number of MTA DMOD threads to handle connections to:

- MDB/XAPI MA Delivery Queue clients
- XAPI MA Retrieval Queue clients
- XAPI MT Gateway clients
- MMI clients

All MTA DMOD threads (of whatever type) can support multiple connections. Connections are load-shared over threads of the same type.

LAN-MTA DMOD threads

Maximum number of MTA DMOD threads to handle connections to LAN-MTAs.

RAS LAN-MTA DMOD threads

Maximum number of MTA DMOD threads to handle RAS connections to remote MTAs.

TP4 control blocks

Maximum number of concurrent TP4 connections supported.

TP4 threads

Maximum number of MTA DMOD threads handling TP4 connections. This is multiplied by two for the two subtypes (Driver, Async Notify) of TP4 threads.

TP4 async notify timeout (msec)

Timeout on select() call for asynchronous notification. This value is the maximum time before the first send/receive on a new connection will be noticed after the connection is established.

TCP/IP control blocks

Maximum number of concurrent RFC1006(TCP/IP) connections supported.

TCP/IP threads

Maximum number of MTA DMOD threads handling RFC1006 connections. This number is multiplied by two for the two subtypes (Driver, Async Notify) of RFC1006 thread.

TCP/IP async notify timeout (msec)

Timeout on select() call for asynchronous notification. This value is the maximum time before the first Send/Receive on a new connection will be noticed after the connection is established.

Eicon wait timeout (msec)

Timeout on x25done() call for asynchronous notification. This value is the maximum time before the first Send/Receive on a new connection will be noticed after the connection is established.

Eicon X.25 result threads

Number of MTA DMOD threads handling EICON X.25 connections.

Eicon X.25 connections

Maximum number of concurrent EICON X.25 connections supported.

XAPI MA threads

Number of threads handling calls from:

- MDB/XAPI MA Delivery Queue clients
- XAPI MA Retrieval Queue clients

XAPI MT threads

Number of threads handling calls from:

- XAPI MT Gateway clients

XAPI MA queue threads

Number of threads handling interaction with the MTA on behalf of:

- MDB/XAPI MA Delivery Queue clients
- XAPI MA Retrieval Queue clients

XAPI MT queue threads

Number of threads handling interaction with the MTA on behalf of:

- XAPI MT Gateway clients

Concurrent XAPI sessions

Maximum number of concurrent connections to:

- MDB/XAPI MA Delivery Queue clients
- XAPI MA Retrieval Queue clients
- XAPI MT Gateway clients

Submit/Deliver threads

Number of MTA Submit/Deliver threads

Dispatcher threads

Number of MTA Dispatcher threads. This is multiplied by three for the three subtypes (Router, Fanout, Result) of Dispatcher thread.

Transfer threads

Number of MTA Transfer threads. This is multiplied by two for the two subtypes (Transfer In, Transfer Out) of Transfer thread.

ds_read cache latency (secs)

Information read from the directory is saved in the ds_read cache. This field determines the cache latency. A higher latency means directory information is read less often, but directory changes may not be noticed until the cache latency time expires.

ds_search latency (mins) for transport stacks

Time interval between directory searches for transport stacks. New transport stacks added to the directory may not be processed until this time interval expires.

RTS threads

Number of platform threads handling the RTSE level of the OSI stack.

Kernel threads

Number of platform threads handling the Presentation and Session level of the OSI stack.

DB data buffers per object

Number of DB Server buffers configured per DB object. More buffers require more memory but make it less likely for a DB object to be rolled out to disk due to lack of buffer space.

DB file handles

Number of DB Server file handles configured. This determines the maximum number of DB files open concurrently. If more Opens are required than the configured value, DB objects will be rolled out to disk.

DB file count delete threshold

DB Server files with a file count greater than this will be deleted once they are finished with. Old unused files are reused, therefore a higher value improves performance by reducing the number of File Delete and Create calls

DB file size delete threshold

DB Server files bigger than this size are be deleted once they are finished with. A higher value improves performance by reducing the number of File Delete and Create calls.

RAM log severity (X.400 Service)

MTA X.400 Service events with a severity equal to or higher than this are logged to the RAM/Termination log. The MTA RAM log is dumped out at termination time.

RAM log severity (Resource)

MTA Resource events with a severity equal to or higher than this are logged to the RAM log.

RAM log severity (Security)

MTA Security events with a severity equal to or higher than this are logged to the RAM log.

RAM log severity (Interface)

MTA Interface events with a severity equal to or higher than this are logged to the RAM log.

RAM log severity (Field Engineering)

MTA Field Engineering events with a severity equal to or higher than this are logged to the RAM log.

RAM log severity (Operator event)

MTA Operator events with a severity equal to or higher than this are logged to the RAM log.

RAM log severity (Configuration)

MTA Configuration events with a severity equal to or higher than this are logged to the RAM log.

RAM log severity (Directory Access)

MTA Directory Access events with a severity equal to or higher than this are logged to the RAM log.

RAM log severity (Operating System)

MTA Operating System events with a severity equal to or higher than this are logged to the RAM log.

RAM log severity (Internal Processing)

MTA Internal Processing events with a severity equal to or higher than this are logged to the RAM log.

APDU logging required

When set this option logs all APDUs sent or received by the MTA to file.

Flush Results to Disk

Secure message transfer results to avoid duplicate messages being sent after outages. Performance will be improved if results are not secured, but there is a good chance that there will be duplicate messages received by recipients if the MTA terminates unexpectedly .

Number of RAS LAN-MTAs

Maximum number of RAS LAN-MTAs supported by the MTA.

Number of remote sites connected over LAN

Maximum number of remote sites connected over the LAN. This equates to the number of Virtual Domains/Site Connectors in this site.

Number of DLs allowed

Maximum number of DLs supported by the MTA.

X500 DN

Full directory name of the MTA.

DSA Address

Computer name the MTA is running on. This is used to build a Presentation Address for the DSA.

MTA Run Directory

Runtime directory for Exchange Server components, usually C:\Exchsrvr.

Max concurrent XAPI applications

Maximum number of concurrent XAPI applications. This is summed together with the existing registry parameters for maximum number of LanMta connections and Administrator clients to give the total number of LTAB entries, that is, the maximum number of (duplex) connections to/from other servers.

Max RPC calls outstanding

Maximum number of RPC threads. This limits the maximum number of RPC procedure calls that are guaranteed to be able to be processed at one time. Used by RpcServerUseAllProtSeqs() and RpcServerListen().

Min RPC Threads

Minimum number of RPC threads. This identifies the minimum number of call threads. Used by RpcServerListen().

RPC Authentication Level

RPC authentication level. This identifies the level of authentication to use over outgoing RPC connections.

Dispatch remote MTA messages

Used by development to allow for the replaying of a saved MTA database on a different machine.

Text Event Log

Used to send the Event Log messages to text files as well as to the NT Event Log. Useful for gathering log information for sending back to development upon request.

Handle Exceptions

Forces the MTA to handle unexpected exceptions in the code and dump out debug information. Should only be used when requested by development for tracking a particular problem.

Microsoft Exchange Server Schedule+ Registry Reference

This section provides the details on the registry settings used by Schedule+.

The following rules apply to these registry keys.

- For Boolean keys, zero or no value means false, non-zero means true.
- The default is zero, false, or empty unless otherwise noted.
- Default values are absent from .ini files unless otherwise noted by the comment "(always present)", meaning after exiting Schedule+ online once.
- Supported color values are 1 through 16 inclusive.

Caution You should not change any of the Microsoft Exchange Server registry key values unless you are familiar with the full effect of the change.

Under Registry Key:
Hkey_local_machine\Software\Microsoft\Schedule+\Application

Name	Type	Default Value	Description
AutoScanDisabled	REG_DWORD	0	1–autoscan disabled, 0–autoscan enabled
			Setting this registry key to 1 turns off all background processing of Schedule+ mail, including Auto-Accept, Auto-Delete, Auto-processing of responses (including deletion of silent responses), and Auto-forward (for MS Mail clients).
PollTime		600	Number of seconds between polling intervals.
LocalUser			(Should always be present.)

(continued)

Name	Type	Default Value	Description
LocalPath			Path where the local Schedule+ file exists. (Should always be present.)
AppPath			Path where Schedule+ exe will be found initialized by the setup program, or when App runs.
CDPath			Path where the DLLs are located. Setup program initializes this.
			Will be different from AppPath if the user chooses to install in "Run from CD" mode, in which case we only install the .Exe on the local drive.
OfficeInstalled			Set to 1 if Schedule+ was installed with Microsoft Office.
MailDisabled			Do not attempt to load and start MAPI and open a server file
FormsRegistered			Indicates that the MAPI forms have been registered.
ServerPath			Path to server, for example, \\davewh5server\po
TransportList			Name of transport list, for example, Xpt.xpt
ScheduleFinders			Names of transport DLLs, such as Mstre
ScheduleInterfaces			Names of interface DLLs, such as Msscd
DefaultLocalPath			Primer path for 'choose local path' dialog at initialization time.
PrimaryServer			Indicates whether you should give the user the option to choose a local file.
WatchInstalled			Indicates watch export DLL installed.
OptionsTab			The last options tab selected by user.

(continued)

Name	Type	Default Value	Description
OptionsFilePath			If this exists, it must be a valid path that points to a VUE file. Otherwise, the username is used to create a VUE file that resides in the Windows directory.
RecoverAll			Indicates that header errors should be treated as file corruptions rather than version errors. When the file header is corrupt the file may look like it is not a Schedule+ file. Normally the code treats this as a foreign file type and does not try to recover the file. When this key is set to 1, the code treats the file as if it were corrupt.
ApptBookLinesColor			
GridLinesColor			
GridTextColor			
TentativeApptColor			
Ex-Import Stuff			
ExportRange			Default: All (entire file)
ImportNoDupCheck			If set to 1, greatly speeds up CSV imports by not checking for duplicates.
ImportNoDupCheck			k ; if ; if set to 1, greatly speeds up CSV imports by not checking for duplicates
ImportDoNotAsk AboutConflicts			
ArchiveFile			Archive path/filename
ExportFile			Most recent export path/filename
ReminderToTop			Default: 5 (in minutes) to bring reminders to top, range 1 - 60 inclusive
SchdplusReminder			Default: ".\Msremind.wav" (name of reminder wave file)
NewTaskGridIgnoreNo DueDate			Whether to exclude tasks with no due date (useful for daily reminder)

(continued)

Name	Type	Default Value	Description
GridAutoFit			Resize columns to fit when resizing window/grid
DemosEnabled			Whether to allow Demos menu command
DefaultPrinter			Was the last printer used the default printer? 0/1
LocalPrintFileDir			Points to the location of the .prt files. no default!
GrayShade			Default: 230 range is 0 (black) to 255 (white)
PCLGrayPercent			Default: 15 range is 0 to 100 (%)
NoHPTypeLines			
NoToolBar			
NoStatusBar			
CoverBitmap			Path to Windows bitmap file
UpdateCover			Default: 120 (in minutes) between updates of cover page
NoNewContactSpaceJump			Don't jump from first to last name on space in new contact
DefaultNetPassword			Default: no default password
SyncStartIdle			Default: 6000 number of csecs to wait after a user action before continuing synchronization
PrimaryServer			Default: 0. Working primarily from Server file? This flag only reflects the default setting for new users on the machine. If the user changes this setting, the change will be saved in the profile, not the registry.
ShowRecurInstances			Default: 1 (most 32)
InitialAccess			Default: 0 (read_minimal) 1 = none, 2 = read
[Watch Wizard]			

(continued)

Name	Type	Default Value	Description
PhoneShowNormal		0	Shows names normally (for example, "first last" instead of "last, first"). Note that in most cases we want to show "last, first" because the Watch sorts the textized string that we send it.

[Microsoft Schedule+]

PollTime			Default: 6000 (in centiseconds)
DefaultRemindAgain=			
DefaultRemindAgain Amount			Default: 5
DefaultRemindAgain Units			Default: minutes

Customizing Menus

The following is an example of a customized menu printout.

[Custom Menus]

```
;Examples
NewMenu=2.0;help;Sample;;;Status for sample;helpfile.hlp;0
NewCommand=2.0;Sample,#-1;Schedule+ Ini;;notepad schdplus.ini;Edit
Schedule+
Ini file;helpfile.hlp;0
Sep=2.0;Sample,#-1;;;;;;
tag=version;menu to precede;new menu;DLL name;command string;status
string;help
file;help id
tag Identifies the command to someone reading the INI file,
but serves no other purpose.
version Identifies the version of Schedule+ with which the
command is compatible; 2.0 is the current version.
menu to precede Path to an existing menu. The new menu item will be
added before the menu. The name is case insensitive,
and ampersands are ignored. Commas are used to
specify the path to the menu. To specify an absolute
menu position use '#' followed by the number for the
position. If -1 is specified for the position then
the new menu will be added at the end of menu
specified.
```

new menu The menu name to be added to the menu bar. As usual,
you may include an ampersand just before the letter
that is to serve as an ALT-key accelerator. If no
name is provided, then a seperator will be added.
DLL name Name or path of the DLL in which the custom command
resides. (DLL not currently supported)
command string Command string passed as one of the parameters to
the DLL entry point for the command. If no DLL name
then the command string will be used to call WinExec.
If no command string or DLL name is provided, then a
new pop-up menu will be added.
status string String displayed on the status bar when the menu item
is selected.
help file Windows help file to be invoked when the user presses
F1 while the command is selected. Passed to the
Windows Help program.
help id Passed to the Windows Help program along with the
help file name. Use -1 (help file index) if there is
no specific entry in the help file for this command.

Deleting Menus

[Deleted Menus]

```
;Examples
DeleteHelp=2.0;help
DeleteUndo=2.0;edit,undo
tag=version;menu path
```
tag Identifies the command to someone reading the INI file,
but serves no other purpose.
version Identifies the version of Schedule+ with which the
command is compatible; 2.0 is the current version.
menu path Path to an existing menu to be removed. The name is
case insensitive, and ampersands are ignored. Commas
are used to specify the path to the menu. To
specify an absolute menu position use '#' followed by
the number for the position.

Creating Custom Pop-up Menus

[Custom Popup Menus]

```
;Examples
NewCommand=2.0;toolbar,#-1;Schedule+ Ini;;notepad schdplus.ini;Edit
Schedule+
Ini file;helpfile.hlp;0
tag=version;menu to precede;new menu;DLL name;command string;status
string;help
file;help id
```

Note Same format as [Custom Menus] section, but use one of the following names.

For pop-up menus:

- edit, appointments, events, tabs, toolbar, tasks, projects, contacts, columns, navigator

[Deleted Popup Menus]

```
;Examples
DeleteApptCut=2.0;appts,cut
tag=version;menu path
```

Microsoft Exchange Server Internet Mail Service Registry Reference

This section provides details on the registry settings used by the Internet Mail Service.

Under Registry Key:
SYSTEM\CurrentControlSet\Services\MSExchangeIMC\Parameters

Name	Type	Default Value	Description
ArchiveFailedMessage Settings	REG_DWORD		
AssertState	REG_DWORD		
BadInMessageAction	REG_DWORD	0x1	Set this registry parameter to 1 to save inbound messages that cannot be processed by the Internet Mail Service and have non-delivery reports (NDRs) created to a BAD directory under the IMCDATA\IN directory.

(continued)

Name	Type	Default Value	Description
BadOutMessageAction	REG_DWORD	0x1	Set this registry parameter to 1 to save outbound messages that cannot be processed by the Internet Mail Service and have NDRs created to a BAD directory under the Imcdata\out directory.
CommonName	REG_SZ	Internet Mail Service (zoomflume)	
ConsoleStatFrequency	REG_DWORD	0x14	Controls how often (in seconds) status is printed to the console; only relevant in console mode.
Debug	REG_DWORD	0	Sets the Internet Mail Service's internal debug level
DebugBoxState	REG_DWORD		
DisplayMessageStats	REG_DWORD	0x1	Controls what stats are displayed in console mode.

(continued)

Name	Type	Default Value	Description
DisableLoopback Connections	REG_DWORD	0	The Internet Mail Service allows configurations where SMTP connections are made to itself. There are cases where this behavior is desired, such as when one Microsoft Exchange user addresses another using an SMTP proxy. However, this can also allow loopbacks and inefficient configurations. You can configure the Internet Mail Service so it won't initiate SMTP connections if the destination host's IP address matches its own. Instead, it will create an NDR for the message. To enable the Internet Mail Service's connection loopback detection, set the DWORD registry value to 1.
DisableResolver SearchList	REG_DWORD	0	If you are using a wildcard MX DNS record, the Internet Mail Service will append the default domain from your TCP/IP configuration to each host name before trying to resolve it in DNS. To prevent this, set the DisableResolverSearch List value to 1. This setting stops the Internet Mail Service from appending a domain to host names before trying to resolve them.

(continued)

Name	Type	Default Value	Description
DiskSpaceLowWater Mark	REG_DWORD		If disk space falls below this number the Internet Mail Service will enter flush mode until it increases above this number.
EnableMIMEWrap	REG_DWORD	0	EnableMIMEWrap controls word-wrap in outgoing non-TNEF MIME messages. If it is enabled, lines in MIME messages are wrapped at a fixed column. If EnableMIMEWrap is disabled (and UseRTFText is also disabled), lines are wrapped using quoted printable encoding. MIME-enabled readers will unwrap the lines, restoring the original text flow, but users with non-MIME readers will see a "=" character appended to each wrapped line of text. EnableMIMEWrap is enabled by default.
			UseRTFText also affects word-wrap. If enabled, text lines in all non-TNEF messages are wrapped at a fixed column, regardless of the setting of EnableMIMEWrap. The word-wrap setting for non-MIME messages on the Internet Mail Service properties in the Microsoft Exchange Server Administrator program is ignored.

(continued)

Name	Type	Default Value	Description
ExtensionDLL	REG_SZ	c:\exchsrvr\ connect\ msexcimc\bin\ imcext.dll	Pointer to an Internet Mail Service message routing extension DLL. This value should exist only if an extension DLL is used.
GoodInMessageAction	REG_DWORD		
GoodOutMessage Action	REG_DWORD		
HomeDSA	REG_SZ	Internet Mail Service (zoomflume)	
IgnoreCommaInFrom	REG_DWORD		If non-zero, unquoted display names with commas are supported in addresses (for Xenix compatibility).
InboundCanonicaliza- tion	REG_DWORD	0x1	Obsolete. Not used.
InboundEmailAddress List	REG_MULTI_ SZ	SMTP	Internet Mail Service proxy type.
InboundThreads	REG_DWORD	0x1	Number of threads dedicated to inbound processing.
InOutThreads	REG_DWORD	0x6	Number of threads dedicated to both inbound and outbound processing.
MAPIDeferredErrors	REG_DWORD		
MaxReceivedHeaders	REG_DWORD	0x12	Maximum number of hops a message can take before being returned as non-deliverable. This prevents infinite loops from occurring. The number is the count of received headers in the message.
MaxRecipients	REG_DWORD	0	Maximum recipients in a batch
MessageTracking	REG_DWORD	0	Obsolete. Not used.

(continued)

Name	Type	Default Value	Description
NoExceptionHandling	REG_DWORD		If present and non-zero, exception handling is disabled
ObjectDefaultPerformanceData	REG_BINARY		
ObjectGUID	REG_SZ	61DF5950-E40A-11ce-A2C9-00AA0040E865	
Organization	REG_SZ		
OrgUnit	REG_SZ		
OutboundThreads	REG_DWORD	0x1	Number of threads dedicated to outbound processing
OutQueueHighWater Mark	REG_DWORD	0x61a8	When this many messages are queued in the OUT directory, the Internet Mail Service will stop accepting messages.
OutQueueRestartWater Mark	REG_DWORD	0x3a98	If the Internet Mail Service has stopped accepting messages due to the high water mark being reached, and when the number of messages in the Out directory falls below this number, the Internet Mail Service will start accepting messages again.
PS_ROUTING_Xlate	REG_DWORD		
QueueWaitTimeout	REG_DWORD		
RootDir	REG_SZ	d:\Exchsrvr\imc data	
RouteRecalculation Interval	REG_DWORD	0xf	Controls how often the Internet Mail Service checks for GWART updates; if zero it never checks.
SaveBeforeSubmit	REG_DWORD		

(continued)

Name	Type	Default Value	Description
SaveFailedOutbound	REG_DWORD		If non-zero, outbound messages failing content conversion that have NDRs created are stored in the Content Conversion Failed folder.
SiteDN	REG_SZ	/o=Lazy_D/ ou=Istanbul	
SiteDomain	REG_SZ		The domain to be used in the originator address for reports generated by the Internet Mail Service. Overrides the site address.
SMTPRecvTimeout	REG_DWORD	0x12c	SMTP protocol timeout waiting for packet transmission. To never time out, this number can be set to zero. However, this is not recommended because it could cause the Internet Mail Service to stop responding.
SMTPWaitForAck	REG_DWORD	0x12c	SMTP protocol timeout for OK response to a command sent to another host (seconds).
SMTPWaitForBanner	REG_DWORD	0x12c	SMTP protocol timeout for HELLO banner from another host (seconds).
SMTPWaitForData Block	REG_DWORD	0x258	SMTP protocol timeout waiting for the other host to send the CRLF termination to the data block.
SMTPWaitForData Initiation	REG_DWORD	0x78	SMTP protocol timeout waiting for the other host to start transfer of the data block.
SMTPWaitForData Termination	REG_DWORD	0x258	SMTP protocol timeout waiting for a response from the other host to the CRLF data termination.

(continued)

Name	Type	Default Value	Description
SMTPWaitForMail From	REG_DWORD	0x12c	SMTP protocol timeout waiting for a response to the Fröm command.
SMTPWaitForRcpt	REG_DWORD	0x12c	SMTP protocol timeout waiting for a response to the Rcpt command
ThreadsPerProcessor	REG_DWORD	0x3	
UseRTFText	REG_DWORD	0x1	UseRTFText specifies if reply-and-forward text is quoted in outgoing non-TNEF. If it is enabled (non-zero), Internet-style quoting is applied to reply-and-forward text by inserting a greater-than sign (>)before each line. If UseRTFText is disabled (set to zero or not present), no Internet-style quoting is applied. UseRTFText is enabled by default.
WarnedAboutTCPIP Config	REG_DWORD	0x1	

Microsoft Exchange Server Setup Registry Reference

This section provides the details on the registry settings used by the Microsoft Exchange Server Setup program.

Caution You should not change any of the Microsoft Exchange Server registry key values unless you are familiar with the full effect of the change.

Under Registry Key:
HKEY_LOCAL_MACHINE\SOFTWARE\MICROSOFT\EXCHANGE\ SETUP

Name	Type	Description
InstallPath*	REG_SZ	The path to the last install point.
Services*	REG_SZ	The path to Microsoft Exchange services.
MSMailConnector*	REG_SZ	Same as Services.

(continued)

Name	Type	Description
Internet*	REG_SZ	Same as Services.
X400*	REG_SZ	Same as Services.
Sample Applications*	REG_SZ	The path to the Sample Applications public folder.
Books Online*	REG_SZ	The path to the on-line documentation.
AdminDest*	REG_SZ	The path to the Administrator program.
Build	REG_DWORD	The build number of the setup executable that was run last.

* These keys exist only if the component is installed.

Microsoft Exchange Server System Attendant Registry Reference

This section provides details on the registry settings used by the System Attendant.

Caution   You should not change any of the Microsoft Exchange Server registry key values. Severe system problems might occur! You can change some values through the Administrator program. Some values (such as Enterprise, Server, and Site) cannot be changed.

Under Registry Key:
H_KEY_LOCAL_MACHINE/System/CurrentControlSet/
ServicesMsexchangeSA/Parameters

Name	Type	Description
Enterprise		The Microsoft Exchange Server enterprise name.
LogDirectory		The directory for Message tracking log file.
LogFlushFreq		The number of log entries to wait for before writing a message tracking log file to the disk.

(continued)

Name	Type	Description
OldLogsCleaningInterval(Days)		The number of days old message tracking log files will be kept before deleting.
MaintenanceMode/Flag		Indicates if maintenance mode is on or off. In maintenance mode, the server monitor will not attempt to restart stopped services. You can enter maintenance mode using the Administrator program command line. For more information, see the Administrator's Guide under "Stopping Monitors for Maintenance."
MaintenanceMode/User		Indicates the user who last changed the maintenance mode.
MaintenanceMode/Time		Indicates the time at which the maintenance mode was last changed.
Polling Interval		The delay in milliseconds between times the System Attendant does scheduled tasks.
Server		The Microsoft Exchange Server name.
Site		The Microsoft Exchange Server site name.

Microsoft Exchange Server Information Store Registry Key Structure

The following diagram shows the keys created in the registry when the information store is installed by Microsoft Exchange Server Setup.

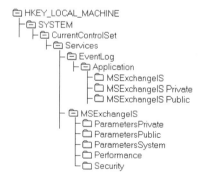

Microsoft Exchange Server Information Store Registry

Key/Value Hierarchy

EventLog\Application

        MSExchangeIS

                CategoryCount

                CategoryMessageFile

                EventMessageFile

                Types Supported

        MSExchangeIS Private

                CategoryCount

                CategoryMessageFile

                EventMessageFile

                Types Supported

        MSExchangeIS Public

                CategoryCount

                CategoryMessageFile

                EventMessageFile

                Types Supported

MSExchangeIS

                DependOnGroup

                DependOnService

                DisplayName

                ErrorControl

                ImagePath

                ObjectName

                Start

                Type

(continued)

ParametersPrivate

Clean Per User Read Interval

DB Path

Disabled

General Event Log

Log Downloads

Reread Logon Quotas Interval

Track Duplicates

Transport Event Log

ParametersPublic

DB Path

Disabled

General Event Log

Log Downloads

Maximum Cached Categorizations

Maximum Cached Restrictions

Read PF Instances Interval

Read PF Settings Interval

Replication

Replication Backfill Timeout
(Solicited)

Replication Backfill Timeout
(Unsolicited)

Replication DS Updates

Replication Event Log

Replication Expiry

Replication Folder Count Limit

Replication Message Count Limit

Replication RMR Timeout

Replication Send Folder Tree

Replication Status Updates

Replication Timeout

Track Duplicates

Transport Event Log

(continued)

ParametersSystem

>Aging Clean Interval
>
>Aging Keep Time
>
>Circular Logging
>
>DB Log Path
>
>DB Recovery
>
>DB System Path
>
>DS Computer
>
>Max Threads
>
>MTA Computer
>
>Online Compaction
>
>Reread GWART Interval
>
>Reread IS Quotas Interval
>
>Synch Mailbox/Check OOF Interval
>
>This Server
>
>Working Directory

Performance

>Close
>
>Collect
>
>First Counter
>
>First Help
>
>Last Counter
>
>Last Help
>
>Library
>
>Open

Security

>Security

CHAPTER 7

Troubleshooting Microsoft Exchange Server

This chapter discusses ways to troubleshoot or prevent certain problems in your organization. It is organized into the following sections:

- Improving TCP/IP Startup Times
- Accessing the Registry After Problems Are Reported
- Backing Up Inbox Assistant Rules

Improving TCP/IP Startup Times

When starting the Microsoft Exchange Client, one of the more common reasons for slow startup is the failure to resolve the Microsoft Exchange Server Transport Control Protocol/Internet Protocol (TCP/IP) host name. This section outlines a procedure for eliminating host name resolution problems on client computers running TCP/IP.

Note Before troubleshooting TCP/IP, make sure the Microsoft Exchange Client is not running.

▶ **To troubleshoot TCP/IP**

1. In Control Panel, double-click the **Mail** icon.

2. In the **Services** tab, select **Microsoft Exchange Server**.

3. Choose **Properties**.

4. In the **General** tab, type the correct Microsoft Exchange Server name and the mailbox name.

5. Choose **Check Name**.

After you have verified that the server name and mailbox name are correct, and choose **Check Name**, you can determine how much time it takes to resolve the name. If it takes more than 30 to 40 seconds to resolve the name, read the following sections to improve startup times.

Improving Startup Times

To improve startup time and performance, follow the steps below, keeping in mind that the host name is resolved in the following order over TCP/IP.

1. Hosts file
2. DNS server
3. NetBios cache
4. WINS server
5. Broadcast
6. LMHOSTS file

Step One: Replace Server Name with IP Address

Use the following procedure to test name resolution and to ping the server computer.

▶ **To replace the server name with an IP address**

1. In Control Panel, double-click **Mail**.

2. In the **Services** tab, select **Microsoft Exchange Server**.

3. Choose **Properties**.

4. In the **General** tab, type the Internet Protocol (IP) address rather than the server name.

5. Choose **Check Name**.

This procedure will test name resolution, and it will also initiate a basic remote procedure call (RPC) ping to the Microsoft Exchange Server computer. The ping utility determines whether a network path can be made between two computers (TCP/IP only).

Microsoft Exchange server:
172.16.16.1

Mailbox:
Bill Lee   Check Name

IP Address Fails to Resolve

If the IP address fails to resolve to the correct Microsoft Exchange Server name, there is either a problem with the RPCs to the Microsoft Exchange Server computer, or with the IP address of the Microsoft Exchange Server computer.

At the command prompt, try to ping the IP address of the Microsoft Exchange Server computer. If this fails, there may be a networking issue or a TCP/IP configuration issue that is preventing connection to the Microsoft Exchange Server computer. This issue must be resolved before the client can connect to the server over TCP/IP.

If a ping of the IP address is successful, but a profile checkname fails to resolve the IP address, then the RPC binding order may be incorrect. Verify that the RPC binding order includes **ncacn_ip_tcp** first in the list.

IP Address Resolves

If the IP address resolves to the correct Microsoft Exchange Server computer name quickly, then continue with Step Two, below.

Step Two: Ping the Server Name (Host Name Resolution Troubleshooting)

At this point, the Microsoft Exchange Server computer is available for connection through the IP address. The next step is to verify the host name resolution. At the command prompt, ping the Microsoft Exchange Server computer name.

Ping Succeeds

If pinging the Microsoft Exchange Server name works in a timely manner, but the Client starts up slowly, the RPC binding order may need to be modified. For more information, see Knowledge Base article Q136516, "Improving Windows Client Startup Times."

Ping Fails

Run IPCONFIG /all (or WINIPCFG on Windows 95) and check for an address in the DNS entry box. The Domain Name Service (DNS) can be set for all TCP clients through the dynamic host configuration protocol (DCHP), or by using the TCP configuration in Control Panel for the individual computers.

Step Three: Ping the DNS IP Address (DNS Configuration Troubleshooting)

If IPCONFIG displays an IP address in the **DNS Servers** box, the client computer is configured to resolve host names through the DNS.

The next step in troubleshooting is to verify that the DNS server is available. At the command prompt, ping the DNS IP address. If the DNS does not respond to the request, additional attempts are made at 5–, 10–, 15–, and 20–second intervals. This is the design of DNS and is usually the cause of slow client startup.

Ping to DNS Server Fails

If the client computer is configured for a DNS server that is not available, then DNS either needs to be disabled or configured for a DNS server that is available at all times.

Ping to DNS Server Succeeds

If the DNS server is available and configured properly, the Microsoft Exchange Server computer name and IP address need to be added to the DNS database. After this is done, pinging the Microsoft Exchange Server computer name will resolve to an IP address by the DNS server, enabling faster startup times of the Microsoft Exchange Client.

Adding the Microsoft Exchange Server Computer to the Hosts File

The Hosts file is read every time a Windows Sockets (Winsock) application attempts to resolve a host name. There are no #PRE options to preload entries (LMHOSTS). You can add the Microsoft Exchange Server entry to the Hosts file and then try again without having to restart Windows. The Hosts file on Windows 95 is located in the Windows directory. On Windows NT, it is located in the Windows\System32\Drivers\Etc directory.

Accessing the Registry After Problems Are Reported

If you encounter an error message that indicates Microsoft Exchange Server cannot access the registry, it is most likely because an incorrect value has been detected in this single instance and the registry couldn't be updated.

To resolve this problem, delete the instance and then add it back.

Note If you are concerned that you might be deleting a critical element from your program, call Microsoft technical support before making any changes.

Deleting the instance removes the old instance and enables you to start over. However, sometimes deleting an instance that has a corrupt registry entry may not be successful. You can follow up by performing the following steps.

1. Stop the external instance from the **Control Panel\Services** dialog box.
2. Remove the instance name from the following registry value:

    CurrentControlSet\NT External\Linkage\Export" MULTI_SZ
3. Delete the following instance key from the registry:

    CurrentControlSet\<Instance Name>

This will completely remove the external instance.

Backing Up Inbox Assistant Rules

You can back up rules that users have specified while using the Inbox Assistant in the Microsoft Exchange Client. In some cases, users have specified a large number of rules in their Inbox Assistant. While these rules are simple to recreate, it is easier to back up the rules after they have been set. Then the rules can be restored as needed.

The following steps describe how to copy all of your Inbox Assistant rules to a personal folder file (.pst). After you complete these steps, you can remove the Personal Folder service and store the .pst file in a safe location. If you lose your Inbox rules, you can restore them from that .pst file.

▶ **To copy your Inbox Assistant rules to a personal folder file (.pst)**

1. Create a .pst file.

2. Create a folder within the new .pst.

3. Select the new folder in the new .pst.

4. From the **Tools** menu, choose **Application Design**, and then select **Copy Folder Design**.

5. In the **Copy Design From** dialog box, select your server Inbox.

6. Select **Rules**.

7. Choose **OK**.

This copies all your Inbox rules to the new .pst. You can now remove the Personal Folder service and store the .pst in a safe location. If you lose your Inbox rules, you can restore them from the new .pst.

Index